A Privileged Life

Remembering My Journey

Delores F. Brisbon

Foreword by David Black, Ph.D., President
Edited by Christopher A. Hall, Ph.D., Chancellor
Eastern University, St. Davids, Pennsylvania

Edited by Chris Hall, Ph.D., Chancellor, Eastern University and Dean Palmer Seminary, St. Davids, Pennsylvania

Scripture references are from the following sources:
The New International Version (NIV), copyright 1973, 1978, 1984 by
the International Bible Society, published by Zondervan, Library of
Congress #200410619; *The Message*, published by NavPress Publishing
Group, copyrighted 2002; and a part of the NIV/The Message Parallel
Bible, copyright 1973, 1978, 1984, published by Zondervan; Women
of Destiny Bible, copyright 2000 by Thomas Nelson, Inc., New King
James Version (NKJV), copyright 1982, Thomas Nelson Publishers,
Nashville, Tennessee.

Quotations are from: *Daily Strength for Daily Needs,* Mary W. Tileston;
The Family Inspirational Library. Publishers Grosset – Dunlop, New
York. Copyright 1884, 1901, 1912, 1982. ISBN-0-448-01639-7. *My
Utmost for His Highest* by Oswald Chambers, edited by James Reimann,
© 1992 by Oswald Chambers Publications Assn., Ltd., and used by
permission of Discovery House Publishers, Grand Rapids MI 49501.
All rights reserved.

ISBN 1453829709

Printed in the United States of America

*This memoir fulfills a promise to
my beloved husband
James LeRoy Brisbon
who entered heaven
November 12, 2004.*

CONTENTS

Foreword
By David Black, President, Eastern University . **i**

Introduction
A journey that detoured, but never changed direction . **v**

My Beginnings . 1
From a shy, strange and introverted child to a
competent woman

Work in Philadelphia . 27
From Head Nurse to Hospital Executive to Successful
Business Woman:
Navigating personal will and relationships
Living out my faith in volunteering

James and Me . 87
A spiritual enhancement

My Journey with Alzheimer's Disease . 107
Commentary by Donald A. Cramp
From rage to thanksgiving

Grief . 133
Healing

Lessons from Life . 147
Everything has consequences

Quotations by Chapter . 150

Acknowledgements . 153

About the Author . 157

FOREWORD

There we were, ten people seated around a marble table in a mahogany walled room that had once held the private library of a prominent Philadelphia family. The accomplished group included leaders from major corporations, healthcare, law, finance, the church, government, and higher education. Our single agenda item was to develop the rules of engagement for embedding a financially exigent seminary in a university. Six of us were members of the university's board and four were board members of the seminary.

As the meeting unfolded, one member of this impressive and focused collection of decision makers emerged as the wisest of us all. By wisest, I mean not only did she demonstrate deep insight into the grieving of the seminary trustees and the financial concerns of those from the university; she expressed remarkable foresight in describing the transformational potential in disfranchised urban neighborhoods of substantive conjunctions between education, economic development, and the church. While listening to her lay out several practical benefits of such a partnership, I penned the words, "Tennyson's Prophecy," in the margin beside my notes. Like the poet, this remarkable woman "dipt into the future far as human eye could see, saw a vision of the world and all the wonder that would be."

That was my first encounter with Delores Brisbon. In the decade since, it has been a privilege to work with her as colleague and friend in pursuit of that important vision. Along the way, I have heard accounts from others of how her knowledge, wisdom, courage, and faith overcame all of the barriers this society would erect, from her start as a gifted African American floor nurse from the deep South to her career's culmination as a senior executive position in one of America's most complex and prestigious university hospitals. This book includes her description of that journey.

The pages that follow also include a memorable love story, one shared by Delores and her beloved James. Their marriage was a model for busy people under normal circumstances, but became truly poignant as they journeyed together through James' Alzheimer's. Delores's perspective on both marriage and Alzheimer's reflects the same wisdom I observed during our first meeting.

The book of Acts introduces readers to an uncommon person who emerged from a church and society beset by prejudice to establish a new standard for people and institutions. Stephen's qualities included (1) a reputation for ethics and justice, (2) a fullness of God's Spirit, (3) a deep faith in the divine and in humankind, (4) a wisdom that would resolve conflicts and solve complex problems, (5) a winsome grace that helped others pursue the good, (6) the power to effect needed individual and social transformation, (7) the gift of teaching and persuasive discourse, and (8) the ability to love during a time of suffering. Delores

Brisbon is a modern Stephen whose story, like his, needs to be told.

When the American population elected Barack Obama as President, he was quick to credit the generation before his for making his great achievement possible. That was Delores' generation. Her own words in this book will do the same for many of the President's generational peers. They will also be a source of wisdom and encouragement for spouses of Alzheimer's victims—and spouses in general. Importantly, they will challenge all of us to continue to give of ourselves even when we fear that there is nothing left to share. There always is. Delores proves the point.

David Black, President
Eastern University
St. Davids, Pennsylvania

INTRODUCTION

"You know exactly how I was made, bit by bit, how I was sculpted from nothing into something."

Psalm 139:15 The Message

James and I were sitting at the Inner Harbor, Baltimore, Maryland, staring into the water where we had gone to celebrate our marriage anniversary. As the water flowed in front of us, James said, "You run along like that water. Write about that." I said, "OK," as I had many times before when he asked me to write about how I "got so much done."

I attempted writing my story many times, but never thought of my work as unique. I am comfortable in my skin and always have been—what I do becomes a part of who I am, and the fact that my work (both professional and spiritual) and my character are so intertwined always stalled my efforts to put my life onto paper. James died November 12, 2004. In the years since his death, his request has become a command, and has been joined by many other voices. Barbara Murphy-Warrington, a mentoree, stimulated me to begin writing with her comment, "We need your story."

This work is a selected autobiography that covers not my entire life, but certain aspects. This story is not about other people, except where a life has influenced mine. My memoir is a testimonial: to the love between James and me; to my faith in God (its nature and centrality to every aspect of my life); to my spiritual evolution and growth; and to the interconnection between my early formation, my love for James, my faith, and my work. While it would be unlike James to have me write my story inclusive of him, there cannot be separation because our love is interwoven into everything I did for more than 50 years.

James always wanted me to write how I could have been reared in an oppressive, segregated environment and emerged free of bitterness and without a sense of entitlement. He was fascinated how a shy, introverted person could have become, in her mid-twenties, a decisive, effective leader and by 49 years of age, a Chief Operating Officer of the Hospital of the University of Pennsylvania, a premier academic medical center in Philadelphia, Pennsylvania. This story is not a rags to riches journey, but a testimony of a life of faith, love, and acceptance of who I am, and a narrative of how I responded to opportunities that fit spiritually with my skills and gifts. My story is about an integrated life, one which matured in wholeness and gratitude, and moved beyond struggles and obstacles by divine grace.

James and I passionately loved each other, a love that grew stronger over time and our maturity. We loved each other's souls, with interwoven spirits, which allowed us to live together with limited discontent. Our love for each other taught us to give up individual old habits for newness with each other, to respect differences, and to embrace personalities. We did not have a desire to change each other. James admired my ability to navigate multiple roles, but cherished most of all, 'my wife.' Loving this strong, stubborn, quiet, serene, grounded man inspired me to be my best self. I wanted to watch over him, to rear children with him, and to be a partner in those things we chose. We decided to live together in our uniqueness, even as we excelled in some areas, and diminished in others. We decided to be married to each other.

Our unified spirits reared well-adjusted children, Edgar and Nancy, and significantly participated in guiding the development of grandchildren, Emily, Abby and Welton. Our relationship grew stronger during a 17 year journey with Alzheimer's Disease, and we did not allow the disease to invade our love. James, comfortable with himself, gave me the freedom to have friends independent of him, to engage and mentor young professionals, and to work in church and community service. He encouraged, supported and enhanced my professional growth and development, without compromising himself.

I met James twenty-five years after I was born in rural, racially segregated Jacksonville, Florida. I am a daughter of hardworking parents, the sixth of eight children. Our large black family was economically poor. We were reared to value God, family, truth, integrity, sharing and helping others. Our family had an abundance of love, food and sharing. I did not know we were economically poor until high school and I recognized my classmates' largess.

In the 1930s, the southern part of the United States embraced, forced, even legislated segregation as a way of life for black people. Because I did not know any better, racism was not a constant thought for me, nor did I ever hear discussion on the topic in our home. My perception of my world as a black child was not shaped by oppression, but was simply what I lived. Schools, housing, churches, modes of transportation, and social venue was structured to assure that races did not mix. For the first twelve years of school I sat in segregated classrooms, and in grades one to nine, I studied from books used first by white students. When I reached high school, our books were new, a thrilling concept. Despite the segregation of the school system, we were taught by exceptionally prepared teachers, who motivated, encouraged and inspired me to use my intellectual gifts. I graduated high school ranking second in a class of four hundred students. I graduated from college, a mature, socially aware, informed, competent professional woman, transformed from a shy, insecure, and frightened child.

Endowed with a discerning inner spirit, I am a private woman with a preference for solitude. From as long as I can recall, there has been an internal direction that caused me to experience life differently than other children my age. In current days, I would be called a "nerd." I spent my growing up years studying for school, reading the Bible, and participating in worship and programs of the church. As an adult, I am selective about how and with whom I spend time.

Formed by scriptures and shaped in the church, my faith is strong. The Bible is the resource for my life. There is no resource which has influenced me as has the Bible, which has informed me on marriage, social relationships and interactions, psychological and political responses, personal and professional development, health and well being. Faith, for me, is an inner sense, belief and trust in a God I cannot see but believe is a living spiritual being. My faith is strengthened by scriptural teachings, and informed by life in the church. Faith is not one glorious success after another, but means living my life day in and day out with a consistent focus on what is needed of me. Having faith does not mean living a perfect life, but living one which has strength to move through struggles, pain and difficulties with peace. "Faith is running quietly along."

Accepting who I am has limited a desire or need to compare myself with others even when similarities are obvious. Each person is unique; we were not produced in mass. To work at being someone else would suggest that God made a mistake. He did not. I don't seek that which I don't have, nor am I jealous of the acquisitions or achievements of others. I celebrate the success of others even when an accomplishment far outpaces my own. I am a no nonsense person; I don't seek approvals or attention, and am not tolerant of waste of any kind.

I have a passion for work which allows me to manage and achieve meaningful outcomes in significant volumes and in various activities. My ability to organize, plan, and complete work is defined by purpose and priorities. I rarely undertake a task not suitable to my gifts and skills, which has freed me of resentment toward work. Work for me is about service, not success, money, position or power. There is no menial work if it helps another at whatever level of an organization.

My first job in which I scrubbed toilets has been as important to me as any time I gave a professional lecture. I have had many jobs: Nursing required me to wash bodies, empty bedpans, change linens, stroke cheeks, cry, nurture and feed others. As an executive, I organized, planned and restructured managements and entire operational systems, developed programs for the construction of multi-million dollar buildings, and led the operations of a complex academic medical center. As I engaged in most of these activities, I kept a marriage happily intact and reared children. These simultaneous responsibilities required me to also be a housewife: to clean, cook and maintain a home for my family. In the latter 20 years, I have advised, coached and assisted executives across several disciplines, led governance retreats, taught Bible, ministered to the elderly and children, and mentored younger professionals.

As much as I like to work, my greatest satisfaction is to motivate, encourage or inspire others to be the best they can be. Julie Winton and Bruce Goldman, former colleagues at the Hospital of the University of Pennsylvania, describe in our chapter on 'Work' a model of how I enhance the skills of others. Work taught me to balance priorities, to practice spiritual disciplines, to worship God, to take care of my physical self, to relax, and, importantly, to develop effective relationships.

Over and over life has taught me the value of connections with family, friends, and advisors—people who care about what I do and feel, and who care about how together we can build effective relationships. My life has been enriched by such relationships that cross age, gender, race, educational background and religious belief. This diversity of bonds has contributed to my mental and spiritual well being. Professionally, my relationships provided a foundation for a consultant business, Brisbon & Associates, which operated for 15 years, and was never required to propose or market a portfolio. The strength of my effective associations also taught me to recognize those that were not. Effective relationships taught me how to end ineffective ones without injury or compromise to an organization, a person or myself. Relationships taught me how to accept counsel from others and how to be guided, supported and chastened.

Along the way, I have experienced racial isolation, hostility, gossip, jealousy and misrepresentation of my intentions. I have been disappointed, even frustrated by some close associates and colleagues, and I have been able to spiritually transcend behavior that offends me and move into forgiveness and tolerance without compromising who I am. Faith has taught me to recognize and accept that which cannot be changed, and to change what I can.

Reverend Samuel D. Robbins, writing in Tileston's "Daily Strength for Daily Needs," speaks to my view of life.

> There is a faith in God, and a clear perception of His will and designs, and providence, and glory, which gives to its possessor a confidence and patience and sweet composure, under every varied and troubling aspect of events, such as no man can realize who has not felt its influences in his own heart. There is a communion with God, in which the soul feels the presence of the unseen One in the profound depths of its being, with a vivid distinctness and a holy reverence, such as no words can describe.
>
> (1812-1882)

Murphy's Law states, "You can't do just one thing,

everything has its consequences." Choices I made determined my destiny. My memoir illustrates choices and decisions I made during specific periods in my life—marriage, work and faith in my journey with James. I hope you, the reader, will gain an inspiration from my story and in some way be encouraged to live and enhance your journey. Writing our story has significantly healed my grief over losing James and perhaps he knew it would.

Delores Flynn Brisbon

Delores F. Brisbon

BEGINNINGS

"Trust in the Lord with all your heart, and lean not on your understanding in all your ways, acknowledge Him, and He shall direct your paths."

Proverbs 3:5, 6 (NIV)

My Childhood

Some people can remember significant details and events of childhood; I cannot. For many years, I searched for understanding looking for events of importance. I settled that my childhood just happened. I absorbed experiences.

I am the sixth child of eight born to Inez Willis Flynn and Welton Flynn. My siblings and I were divided equally by gender: four boys and four girls. My birth order placed me between two brothers—Milton, who was three years older than I, and Bernard, two years my junior. Both of these brothers are now dead, as is my oldest sister, Ceursheary. Five of us live as I write my story: Welton, Willie, Evelyn, Barbara and I.

Our family was economically poor. We lived in a house without electricity, running water, or an inside bathroom.

1

We did not own a car. Positioned on a dirt road named York Street located just off U.S. Highway 1 South, our two-story, gray wood-frame house, the place of my birth, had seven rooms and three porches. I loved this house that provided spaces for me to read undisturbed. Shortly before I entered high school, my parents purchased a smaller house on the opposite side of York Street. Our new home had electricity, running water, a bathroom with a bathtub, three bedrooms, a kitchen, dining and living rooms and porches. My parents stayed in this second house until well after my graduation from college and beyond the birth of my children. Both houses have since been demolished, and the sites converted for commercial purposes.

My Parents

My parents were born in Blackville, South Carolina. When they married, my mother was 19 years old and my father 26. Their marriage extended 56 years, until my mother's death.

When my parents left Blackville, my oldest sister and two older brothers had already been born. The family relocated to St. Augustine, Florida for a time before settling in Jacksonville, Florida. Family legend says my father may have moved to Washington, D.C. for a time while seeking work. The south of the 1920's was a place of racial discrimination, which did not provide work opportunities for unskilled persons. My father was not formally educated.

My mother, Inez Willis, grew up on an asparagus farm in South Carolina, the youngest child in her family. As an adult, she maintained close relationships with her brothers, Mallie and Johnson, and her sister, Ursula. She reconnected with her estranged sister Remelle later, which proved to be pivotal in my own life.

A woman of strong opinions, Momma had strict rules for family life. I can yet hear her early morning prayers and pleas to God about the issues heaviest on her heart. She was a shouting Baptist worshipper who looked forward to Sunday services. Momma willingly gave of herself to her neighbors—cooking, house cleaning when necessary, sitting with families, and assuredly, praying. While her opinions were sometimes difficult to receive, her caring was genuine and loving.

Momma worked hard to keep our home an orderly, clean environment. Our home had scrubbed floors and crisp curtains, the beds were made, the furniture polished, and the rugs vacuumed. The yard was swept clean, free of trash and debris. She did domestic work outside our house and made cakes and pies from our home, which she sold to white families. She also "took in" and completed laundry for white families. Without an electric washing machine, this was grueling work. Momma used a huge pot of water and boiled clothes over a fire to clean them. The clothes were then scrubbed on a corrugated board to remove remaining soil, rinsed, and then placed on a line to dry. She pressed the clothes using irons heated in a pot of coal. This work required a great deal of time as well as a degree of skill to arrive at the appropriate temperatures so as not to damage the clothes. I look back with awe at my mother's capacity to work.

A gifted cook, Momma enjoyed food—and she made sure we had an abundance of it at each meal. Momma created pancakes, cornbread, biscuits, cakes, and pies from scratch. Store bought products were unacceptable. On Sundays, we enjoyed a veritable feast. Momma began preparations on Saturday, and the characteristic Sunday meal included more than one meat or poultry entree, candied sweet potatoes, baked macaroni and cheese, potato salad, and several vegetables. These meals were celebrations for those of us living at home, the church pastor and his wife, and anyone else Momma decided to feed. I adopted Momma's standard for my own life: meals are a time of fellowship and enjoyment, and are regularly treated as celebrations.

Growing up, I experienced Momma with obedient compliance, not conversation. I did not talk back or disagree with her positions, whether I liked them or not. My silence changed in my junior year of college. During my third year as a nursing student, Momma had what doctors believed to be a mild heart attack. I returned home to help care for her, thinking I could use my nursing skills to help her change her lifelong position toward food. She had diabetes and was overweight—both conditions that were actively damaging her heart. I did not change her mind about eating, but learned instead of her will to choose for herself how and what she would do. She chose to do what she wanted and accepted both the joy and pain of her choices. While I wanted her to change her eating habits but could not change her, I did celebrate her attitude and strength.

Our relationship changed after this brief experience. We began to have weekly phone calls. When Edgar was born, she came to take care of me and remained for two months. She taught me how to nurture my child. I was an instructor of obstetrical nursing, but Momma's experience, wisdom, patience, and conversations taught me how to be a parent. Nine years later when we had a second child, James and I honored Momma by naming our daughter for my maternal grandmother—Nancy.

As Momma advanced in age and diabetes took her sight, I visited her frequently. Our relationship became more intimate: The weekly Saturday morning calls were filled with discussions about life's journey. I listened to her hopes for me and my family, as well as her reflections on her lost health and her expectations of heaven. Importantly, I did not hear many regrets. Her conversations with me gave me strength, encouraging me to live my life by making choices and accepting the outcomes of my decisions. In this seventh decade of my life, 35 years after Momma's death, I have become my mother. Her spirit influences who I am, how I establish priorities, develop relationships, and how I respond to joy, loss and pain.

I have limited background information about my father whose name was Welton Flynn. I never knew his sisters or brothers. I remember the death of his father, but have no recollection of his mother except what he told me. We once went to look for his brother in Southern Florida, where Daddy had been told he lived. Though we did not find his brother, and did not know whether or not he was even alive, I did later connect with his brother's children. The lack of connections to his siblings drew my dad close to his nieces and nephews who became faithful and loving towards him.

Daddy was my hero and friend. Tall, handsome, highly

intelligent, and hard working with a presence of dignity, Daddy gave me value as a woman. He was not extroverted or self-important, but quiet and focused, attentive to his family, other people, and work. He encouraged me to excel without reference to gender, reminding me simply, "You can do it." My dad's faith in me has guided me to do that which I choose to do.

Daddy worked three jobs. He provided janitorial services to a Baptist church, a bank, and the post office. These places were located a short distance from each other along the same street. He earned the trust of his employers, and was allowed to work alone in these buildings without supervision. This was an important element of my dad's character as the culture in the south had little value for black people, and especially black men. The south practiced, encouraged, and mandated Jim Crow practices; however, Daddy navigated his jobs without difficulty and earned respect in doing so. His ability to do what was required of him while maintaining self-respect and courage provided a model for me.

I enjoyed a spiritually profound relationship with my Dad who taught me to smile regardless of a situation. His model of relationship development with others, love for his children and grandchildren, and commitment to provide materially for his family formed some of my values. Importantly, my dad taught me the value of self-respect. The relationship I had with Daddy has enhanced and strengthened my associations and connections with men over the course of my life.

The depth and caring that characterized my relationship with my dad echoed in his relationship with my husband and children. Daddy and James had a relationship of love, enjoyment, and sharing. He adored his grandchildren as they did him. Because James and I lived with our children in Pennsylvania, while my parents remained in Florida, Edgar often spent summers with them. Daddy and Edgar developed a close relationship which endured over my father's life. When Daddy moved to Philadelphia after Momma died, Edgar went to Florida and traveled with him to our home. James and Daddy bonded even more. When he became ill, needing daily care, James took care of him.

Daddy died just as I began to advance in my career, but his influence on my development and security as a woman provided the strong foundation.

My Neighborhood

I grew up in a vibrant and small semi-rural community populated by people of tolerance, sharing, and communication. We visited across fences and yards or stopped by as neighbors sat on porches. Neighbors looked out for each other. We knew each other's children and families. There were few strangers.

Of those women who worked, many were domestic workers, performing what was called "day work" for white families. We had a few schoolteachers and two nurses in our immediate neighborhood. Hairdressers and seamstresses worked from their homes.

The men in our neighborhood were yard cleaners, train conductors, Pullman porters, storekeepers, or railroad workers. I cannot recall a doctor or lawyer in our neighborhood.

The barbershop, bar, an eating/entertainment place, and several small stores were all owned by black men. There was also a shoe repair shop on the edge of our area operated by a man of color, though I am not sure that he owned it.

Most of our food shopping was done a distance from our homes, but small food stores owned by white businessmen were closer. Traveling vendors came almost daily to sell eggs, vegetables, fruit, fish and ice. Some homes had electrical refrigeration; our first house did not.

The men and women of the neighborhood took an interest in our development and many were not reluctant to inform our parents when they believed we were out of line. The moral character development of the neighborhood children was a community effort, with a particular emphasis on us learning to respect both others and ourselves. People in our community were accepted and respected for who they were, not what they did. Character, not social status, was the basis for a relationship, even in the context of employment.

Church

My spiritual formation began in Jerusalem Baptist Church, located a short distance from our home. Many people in our neighborhood attended or were members of a church. At that time, churches enjoyed esteemed value, a special place, a sacred mission, and were populated with flawed and loving people. Church was a place where we could exhibit our best selves and our worst sides, where we were chastised, and where we were forgiven.

Our neighbors did not discuss religion, nor did they show duplicitous behavior—you were either in the church, on the edge of it, or outside of it. If you were outside, someone hoped or tried to get you in a church. Faith in God was the sustaining force. In spite of discrimination and segregation, we had a freedom of spirit. I cannot remember words such as "stress" or "depression"—rather, people spoke of "faith," "prayer," and insisted, "God will provide." I spent my Sundays in church. We began with Sunday School, and worship extended throughout the afternoon with two or more services. For our worship service at Jerusalem, sermons focused on God and His love, providing a message of direction to us. Our preachers were not seminary-trained or highly educated, but their delivery of sermons was robust and filled with spiritual insights. Christian education was not a label, but a consistent and intentional process.

Momma was a presence in Jerusalem for as long as I can remember. Like the other women of her time, Sunday was a day to dress in her best clothes and take a seat in the front of the church. Daddy started coming to the church when I was eleven years old. He loved the scripture, and spent considerable time listening to his children read to him. His integration into the life of the church progressed quickly. Daddy became the Chairman of the Board of Trustees and a Deacon, and earned admiration from others as he did from me.

One church member in particular, Mrs. Adeline Brown, a domestic worker who was not formally educated, had a heart of love, wisdom, courage and vision. I cannot articulate the effect Mrs. Adeline had on my life, the way she nurtured my soul and encouraged my studies of Scripture, attendence at school, and service in community. Mrs. Adeline frequently talked to me about the "power of God." I accepted and believed what she told me, but I did not feel any change in myself, nor did I feel a need for one. I cannot say that I understood sin, or that I prayed. I knew what was expected of me.

I "joined" the Church during an annual revival service when I was eleven years old. While I had attended church my entire life and read the Scripture from the age of four, I had not yet publicly acknowledged Jesus Christ, nor had I been baptized. Jerusalem Church conducted annual revival services that gave Christians an opportunity to renew their spiritual life, encouraged people to accept Christ, and helped to grow the membership. Coming to Christ meant making a commitment to love and serve others; it meant a repentance of sin, and a spiritual conversion. A dedicated pew of our church was called the "mourners's bench," and those of us who had not repented of our sins sat on these seats. When Mrs. Adeline told me it was time to give my heart to Christ and to shake the preacher's hand, I did. This, however, was an act of obedience to Mrs. Adeline; I did not experience a conversion. It would be years before I understood what my decision meant.

I was baptized, but did not feel different. Immersion under water chilled my body, but I did not experience a spiritual change. What I do recall—an image so clear that it remains in my mind to this day—is Mrs. Adeline, with arms raised and a solemn expression of "Thank You Jesus." It was important, even critical, to Mrs. Adeline to care for and nurture my soul. Her spiritual teachings were a gift, and it was her guidance that helped to form my love for the church. She has been dead many years, but the gift of her spirit remains with me. She was an ordinary woman who lived an extraordinary life—one that mattered, especially to me.

Church in the early years of my life was Jerusalem: its culture and its people. This congregation provided me with a model on how to live my faith. Among our people, I observed tolerance, personal struggle, sadness, sharing, and celebration. While I did not have a profound understanding about any of this at the time, as I matured I recognized that my values of faith were formed by those experiences.

The Formative Years

The social, economical, political, and transportation systems in the south in the 1930's were structured to assure segregation. Housing, theatres, schools and churches were separate. Races did not mix, and opportunities were limited. Because I did not know any better, it was a way of life. We did not have discussions in our home, at least within my hearing, about racial inequality. We did not challenge these conditions.

I began school at six years of age, the mandated age for a first grader in 1939 Duval County, Florida. Because my birth date is in February, I was placed in a mid-term cycle at five years and seven months the prior September. Kindergarten or pre-school was not an option for a black child.

We had one school on our side of town, which served grades one to nine. There was not a high turnover rate among our teachers, which allowed them to form intimate relationships with our parents. An entire family of children could be taught by the same teacher in a certain grade. The stability of these relationships built a culture of strength for my childhood educational development.

These parent-teacher relationships created an environment of learning which motivated, enlightened, and nurtured my educational formation. My early education served to develop my skills, discipline my study methods, change my behavior, and stimulate my mind. My teachers in grades three to nine contributed to who I am as a lifelong student. Mrs. Black, Mrs. Montgomery, Mrs. Timberlake, Mr. Jones and Mr. Avery gave me priority attention. I achieved academically without significant assistance from my teachers, but they enhanced my social skills, and helped me to develop an appreciation for my intellect.

The only high school for black children in Jacksonville, Florida in the 1940s, Stanton High School, was located a distance from our home, and could only be reached by car or bus. The county provided a bus from our elementary school to Stanton High School, but did not make stops to pick up children along the way. I would have needed to go to our elementary school daily to get the bus. My Dad considered the back and forth unacceptable and decided I would use public transportation. I had to walk a distance from the point I got off the bus on both ends of the trip, which was not problematic during the mornings but proved a challenge after school. I could not participate in after school activities or develop relationships outside the classroom. The expense of the bus rides was a hardship on my family financially and discouraged several of my classmates from my side of town from attending school at all, which limited my relationships with those who lived nearest to my home.

I lived in my head. In spite of being alone, I cannot remember feeling loneliness. Social isolation gave me focus and time to study, read Scriptures, and attend church. My skills in science and mathematics made me a good study partner, especially with boys. My relationships with boys developed around study and equal contribution, forming a comfort level with males that has remained throughout my life. I excelled academically although socially I was a disaster. Our limited finances allowed me to purchase new clothes only occasionally, and when I could shop, I had no idea how to select clothing to enhance my appearance. I did not use make-up, could not dance and remained painfully shy. I was referred to by my peers as a "smart country girl."

I graduated from high school ranking second academically in a class of 400 students. Wilhelmina Bryant was ranked first. Our graduation in February left a sizable time gap before we could enter college in September. With my mid-term graduation, I felt the effect of the age rule set in motion in the first grade.

A Maid

I graduated from Stanton High School in February expecting to go to college in September. In the meantime,

13

I needed a job. Opportunities for jobs were limited for a shy, intelligent, black teenager who lived in her head and had no work experience. Historically, my family did the work available to them—as a domestic, a janitor, a deliveries person, or a yard worker—not positions of influence. We were not positioned in a social, political or business world that could bolster my job search.

My brother Willie had a friend named Nadine Brown who worked at a motel on Philips Highway, U.S. 1. When I told Nadine I needed a job, she invited me to work with her. Our work included changing bed linens, cleaning bedrooms, and scrubbing bathrooms. Our work was not physically demanding, just repetitive, which seemed odd to me at the time. It would be years before I understood that this motel had a clientele given to unfaithfulness. I cannot remember what I was paid, but I will forever remember Nadine's kindness.

My motel job lasted a few months before I was hired to be a maid to a newly married young couple. I don't remember much about this job. I have since forgotten the names of the couple, and can barely recall anything about the husband, but I remember the young wife with affection. Tall in stature, she had a graceful carriage and impeccable, simple taste in clothing. She was newly graduated from college, and the experience had meant a lot to her.

This woman, whose name I cannot recall, taught me by her model how to select clothes, shoes, and jewelry that enhanced appearance. The way she carried her height taught me to celebrate mine. She made a choice to be who she was—a tall woman who was not beautiful—by enhancing what she had been given. The four months I worked for her gave me a sense of personal style and how to use my natural assets to best present myself as stylish and in good taste. From her I learned to present myself as a model of dignity, respectability, order and efficiency. More important, she taught me by example to appreciate my tall body. When I left her employment to go to college, this young, white, wealthy, educated woman encouraged me and gave me gifts of clothing and shoes to take with me. I consider my placement in her home a gift, the plan of God, one I celebrate almost daily with gratitude.

"'For I know the plans I have for you,' declares the Lord, 'plans to prosper you and not to harm you, plans to give you hope and a future.'"

Jeremiah 29:11 (NIV)

College

My choice of a college was not complicated or difficult. We did not have money. My teachers counseled me to attend Tuskegee Institute in Alabama. I don't remember how the college preparations were all completed, but at the decision of my father, I entered the School of Nursing.

Daddy believed his daughters should be economically independent. He guided me to enter teaching or nursing because I would always have work. Neither of these professions was particularly appealing to me, but I didn't know what I might do otherwise. I did not disagree with Daddy and proceeded on the course he chose. Looking back, I believe his decision was divine direction. My professional career evolved in major ways because of nursing. Assuredly, Daddy's encouragement and guidance—indeed his decision—led to financial independence.

When I enrolled in college, Tuskegee University was known as Tuskegee Institute. My college was located in Macon County, Alabama, forty miles from Montgomery, Alabama, and an easy drive from Atlanta, Georgia.

> The school was established in 1880 by an act of the Alabama State legislature, which appropriated $2,000 for teachers' salaries, but no funds for land or buildings. This action was led by two men, Lewis Adams, a former slave, and George W. Campbell, a former slave owner, who saw the need for the education of black people in this rural Alabama locale. Booker T. Washington was recruited by a governing board of three men to teach at this newly established institution. He opened the school July 4, 1881 with an enrollment of 30 students. By 1882, Dr. Washington had acquired a 100-acre plantation, which became the landmark of the present campus." (2002 Alumni Directory Tuskegee University)

I traveled from Jacksonville, Florida, to Opelika, Alabama by train, a trip of six hours. My journey is not memorable except for the knot in my stomach caused by a mix of terror, anticipation and aloneness. I was terrified by my first separation from my family, the women from church who had mentored me throughout my childhood, and my community. Unsure of my preparation, I had entered into a world unknown to me, and with limited funds. It was the anticipation of an education which would move me beyond being a domestic worker that balanced my fearful thoughts and motivated me to go forth.

When I arrived on campus that late evening over six decades ago, I could not have imagined how this new home would influence my development. I was assigned a twin bedroom in the nurses' residence that was small by today's standards, and a large shared bathroom situated across a hallway. This arrangement did not present problems as living quarters were gender specified; men did not move beyond the reception desk of the building. Although I had grown up in a large family and sharing space did not present a challenge, the constant presence in the room of a person to whom I was not related proved challenging. Over time, that challenge became instructive rather than intrusive, and I began to mature and learn how to develop relationships. This sharing experience set the pace for me to begin to move beyond shy behavior to social engagement.

In our orientation process, I began to have other revelations about myself. Sitting in a large auditorium listening to the Dean of Women, the late Mrs. Hattie West, I felt alone, but not lonely. Aloneness was becoming my partner. We were separated into two large groups; one group to begin class registration immediately, and the other for additional study—which I now know to be remedial instruction. I was assigned to the group to begin class registration immediately. I was no longer fearful but grateful to my high school teachers for my college preparation.

Worship services at Tuskegee University were held in a beautifully designed chapel said to be constructed with brick made by students of the college. Attendance at chapel on Sunday was a mandate. The student body lined up in formation by schools, with the ROTC and the band leading. Our march began at the cafeteria building, Tompkin Hall, and proceeded to the chapel a fairly short distance away. As a nursing student, I, along with my schoolmates, dressed in professional attire, marched in formation to the chapel. We wore stiffly starched aprons and bibs over grayish blue dresses, clean white shoes buffed to a shine, hose free of runners, and nursing caps properly adorned upon our heads. In cold months, we wore a dark blue cape with a red lining and an insignia on the collar. My cape hangs in my closet to this day, a reminder of an imposed directive to acknowledge God in our student life.

The School of Nursing curriculum at Tuskegee provided an excellent clinical education. The late Dr. Lillian Holland Harvey, the Dean of Nursing, set a standard for my own behavior by her model. The Dean imposed a strict standard about our appearance in public—shoes had to be cleaned, there could be no runners in hosiery, clothing was expected to be starched and fitted, makeup had to be muted, and hair must be properly arranged. As her office was located at the entrance of the Nursing Residence, we could not avoid her appraisal on our way in or out.

Dr. Harvey modeled and taught us respect for who we were and who we were becoming. The clinical experiences we needed to complete our education were not available in sufficient volume to meet licensure requirements at Tuskegee-owned John Andrews Memorial Hospital. Thus our experience had to be obtained away from campus. In the mid-1950s, we were not welcome in southern white hospitals, so Dr. Harvey arranged clinical experiences for us in the northeastern parts of the United States. An entire class could not have been accommodated at one hospital; therefore, we were assigned to different sites.

I spent almost half of my clinical experience in New York City hospitals. I received my medicine, surgery, communicable disease, and pediatrics clinical training either in the Bronx or Brooklyn, New York hospitals. I completed psychiatry and obstetrics in Tuskegee.

While the clinical experience in New York met the requirements of our curriculum, it did even more for my personal growth. These hospitals did not racially discriminate, which meant I had a great many opportunities to live with, learn about, and understand different life styles, backgrounds, cultures, and ethnicities. This experience prepared me clinically to be a nurse and also provided me with another view on life. This assignment began my transition to an understanding, indeed a belief, that I should not be treated differently because of the complexion of my skin. In these New York hospitals, we were taught, assigned, and counseled as nursing students, not as black nursing students.

Dr. Harvey's refusal to expose us to unfair treatment and disrespect taught me responsible leadership. I cannot remember conversations around her decision, but the experience set directions for my life. Her example taught me not to be victim or to complain, but to act with responsive, sensible decisions.

Living and studying in New York exposed me to theater, arts, music, ballet, museums, and other cultural activities beyond the classroom. It also afforded me an opportunity to reconnect my parents to nieces, nephews, and others with whom they had lost personal contact. I returned to

Tuskegee in my senior year socially matured, clinically prepared and significantly less fearful. I had become, over a year and a half, enlightened, open to the reality of racial difference, appreciative of my gifts, and with a new awareness of myself.

In my last year of nursing education, I was privileged to work with a talented and compassionate obstetrician, the late Dr. Joseph Mitchell. Dr. Mitchell treated us as his daughters, seeking to prepare us for adult life. He delivered babies for women of rural Alabama and the Tuskegee neighborhood and faculty. He treated all of these women with equal concern, compassion, interest, honesty, and respect. His example modeled for us not only how to treat patients medically, but how to care for them as well.

In the early 1950s, many Macon County women who arrived at John Andrews Hospital for obstetrics service often had high blood pressure and pre-eclampsia. Many of these women were my age and at-risk for premature delivery. It was clear to me that a great deal of their health outcomes were influenced directly by their social and economic conditions. I began to look at health care as more than illness management; there needed to be preventative health care as well. The knowledge that nutrition, housing, economics, and social status all influenced patient outcomes, which I gained as a student nurse, would inform my later professional nursing decisions, making this early experience in the obstetrical service of John Andrews Hospital a cornerstone for my career.

I witnessed the tragic fire that destroyed the Tuskegee Chapel. This experience caused pain and anger. The chapel burned down at the start of the south's public engagement in the Civil Rights Movement. Though we never knew the true explanation of how the fire started, I speculated it was a statement against those at Tuskegee who were active participants in the fight for equal rights.

My experience at Tuskegee University prepared me professionally, moved me beyond racial limitations, opened my spirit to music and the arts, and strengthened my faith. My education, which began in the segregated system of Duval County, Florida, was transformed in Macon County, Alabama. Tuskegee taught me that education is a process, not just a collection of acquired knowledge. The education I gained at Tuskegee has guided my life -long journey, and the destinations I have reached have been quite surprising. Education required me to find those resources best suited for a situation and use them to leave a place better than when I arrived.

I was socialized in an environment of scholars and achievers at Tuskegee: Dr. Frederick D. Patterson, a President of Tuskegee Institute, was the first President to lead the United Negro College Fund. The work of Dr. George Washington Carver, the distinguished scientist whose research with peanuts is illustrious and acclaimed, stands as a monument for me. Dr. William Dawson, a renowned conductor, musician, and author led the Tuskegee Choir during my time of study. Leaders involved in civil rights were well known among students and provided models for our behavior. Tuskegee's history and its people created an environment for a shy frightened teenager like me to evolve into a secure motivated citizen and, over time, an esteemed professional.

I have learned that success is to be measured not so much by the position that one has reached in life as by the obstacles which he has overcome while trying to succeed. Out of the hard and unusual struggle through which he is compelled to pass, he gets a strength, a confidence that one misses whose pathway is comparatively smooth by reason of birth or race.

Booker T. Washington

A Nurse: John Andrews Memorial Hospital

When I graduated from the School of Nursing at Tuskegee Institute, I accepted a staff nurse position at John Andrews Hospital where I had received some of my clinical experiences as a student. I had successfully completed the State Board of Nursing examination, was licensed to practice and ready to earn. My financial position while studying had not been easy for my family, and I was economically poor.

The city of Tuskegee had become a safe, secure place for me. I planned to stay a year or two at the hospital, a time frame which grew to almost four years. John Andrews Hospital enjoyed a fine reputation in that part of Alabama, attracting patients from as far away as Montgomery, Alabama and Columbus, Georgia. The physicians, most of whom attended Meharry School of Medicine, were highly regarded.

John Andrews did not have a resident physician staff, which afforded nurses the opportunity to work directly and collaboratively with private doctors to plan and manage the care for patients. This relationship enhanced my knowledge and competence and strengthened my skills in communication.

The patient care units in John Andrews Hospital during the early and mid-fifties were organized by gender. We had a male service, female service, obstetrical and newborn unit, pediatric unit and a polio unit which included rehabilitation services. As a young nurse, I gained experiences on all of these units and considerably more in ophthalmology (eye) surgery. I was assigned to the operating room to assist the surgeon, Dr. Horace Wiggins, with eye surgery, and Dr. Joseph Mitchell, the obstetrician, with cesarean sections and gynecological procedures. These clinical experiences advanced my analytical skills, strategic thinking, and ability to plan care for patients in the hospital and beyond. I learned how to both lead and follow other nurses, which developed collegial relationships. John Andrews Hospital had about 225 beds at the time, making it a small, close community, limiting competitiveness;,and enhancing collaboration. This healthy environment allowed me the freedom to lead and move with single focus—patient care.

My willingness to work and accept any assignment earned me promotions, not necessarily in title, but in responsibilities, which gave me my start in administration. My enjoyment of work, compliant behavior, competent service and good relationships led a colleague to recommend me for a position as Director of Nursing at Flint-Goodridge Hospital in New Orleans, Louisiana.

Flint-Goodridge Hospital

A dietician whose name I cannot recall had accepted a position at the now closed Flint-Goodridge Hospital in New Orleans, Louisiana, after leaving John Andrews Hospital in Tuskegee. She recommended to Mr. Clifton Weil, President of Flint-Goodridge Hospital, that he hire me to be Director of Nursing Service. Mr. Weil interviewed me by telephone. I don't recall sending a résumé or even if I had one at that time. We did not discuss position responsibilities, nor did I complete an application, but we did agree on a salary and a starting date, and I accepted the position of Director of Nursing.

I had never been to New Orleans, Louisiana, nor had I heard of Flint-Goodridge Hospital. I only knew the dietician who recommended me. When I prepared to leave Tuskegee, sadness overwhelmed me, and my cousin, the late Charles Willis, tried to get me to back out. But I had given my word, and although doubtful and fearful about my decision, I moved forward. Charles helped me pack and took me to New Orleans where he said goodbye to me at the door of my new home. I felt panic.

At the time Flint-Goodridge Hospital was a pillar and source of pride in the African American community of New Orleans. Like many hospitals across America that served black and poor patients in the late 1950s, survival was difficult. The need to compete with larger, better resourced institutions for doctors had become a major issue, and many small institutions were struggling to stay in business. The lack of finances at Flint-Goodridge Hospital over an extended time period resulted in a poorly maintained facility, outdated equipment, an overworked and underpaid work force, and a struggling public image. A seasoned professional would have seen these conditions immediately. I did not. At that point in my career, I did not have experience, training or exposure to recognize these issues and most assuredly could not address them.

My lack of preparation for this leadership position led me to incorrectly determine that the limited quality of nursing service delivered to patients was the result of inadequate nursing performance. In fact, the nurses' performance was influenced by a systematic deficit, structural financial losses, and less than effective hospital leadership. These nurses were loyal, continuing to work extended hours in less than optimal conditions. The nurses' desire was to keep a job and to save the hospital. Blinded by inexperience, I missed the gravity of the hospital's situation and the loyalty of these women.

Despite my lack of preparation to lead the Nursing Department and my narrow administrative focus, my nursing education, prior clinical experience and leadership ability did improve care to the patients, enhance clinical experience for student nurses, and provide a ray of hope for physicians. These achievements were accomplished at great cost to my spirit. Every encounter with the nursing staff resulted in defensive, hostile behavior toward me. These nurses resented and disliked me, which manifested in the disdain in their tone towards me, sabotage of my work, and misrepresentations of my actions. I believed I was improving the delivery of patient care, designing systems, and developing policies. The nurses viewed me as young, over-educated and not experienced enough to be their leader.

Because of these circumstances, I lived in stressful fear, rejection and aloneness. My only support came from Marguerite Rucker, a member of the Dillard University faculty and the late Margaret Ziegler, the Operating Room Supervisor at Flint-Goodridge. Mr. Weil, the person who hired me, seemed not to like me, and limited his contact with me, including administrative conversations. After eighteen months I resigned, ashamed, sad and disappointed. My entrenched sadness made me physically ill and I moved to Florida to spend time with my family.

I realized soon after arriving in Florida that this would not be my home, but I needed time to discern what I might do. Several weeks of reflection, a hospitalization and surgery allowed me to accept my part in this failed experience. Pride, an extended opinion of my ability, and trusting someone without personally checking the information lead to failure. I had limited experience and no wisdom to guide me. I had lost my spiritual compass. During long periods of solitude, I gained clarity on the danger of flattery, and of not using my inner sense to guide me. My Momma said, "Your conscience" had not been heard. Proverbs 3:7a (NIV) helped me: "Do not be wise in your own eyes." Over time, the confusion and sadness diminished, and I began to focus and look forward to a future.

My mother's sister, Remelle, came to Florida to visit, and over many conversations helped me to see my mistakes and guide me toward healing. Aunt Remelle advised to "put all this" behind me. She invited me to come to Philadelphia, Pennsylvania and live with her. I accepted Aunt Remelle's invitation, and a new life began to emerge.

Delores F. Brisbon

MY WORK IN PHILADELPHIA

*"Give God the best He has given you and be careful
what you do with the best you are given."*

Oswald Chambers

I love to work. I cannot imagine my life without work.
Even so, it seemed highly unlikely that my path as a
black girl born in the early 1930s in the segregated south,
educated in a discriminatory public school system, studying from used books, and graduating from a black college
would lead to the Ivy League Hospital of the University of
Pennsylvania, commonly known as HUP. On November
1, 1979, twenty years after I began work at HUP as a head
nurse, Dr. Edward S. Stemmler, then Dean of the School
of Medicine of the University of Pennsylvania greeted me
with, "Dee, I wanted to be the first to congratulate you
on your appointment as the Administrator," the title for
the Chief Operating Officer. Standing in the door of our
Planning Office, Dr. Stemmler announced to me that the
late Mark S. Levitan, Chief Executive Officer of HUP,
had made a historic decision by appointing the first black
person to lead the operations of HUP.

Ed's announcement to me that morning in 1979
marked a major change in my life. I had navigated earlier

experiences of racism at HUP and had earned successive promotions during some of the worst racial turmoil in American history. My appointment broke the model for hospital leadership. In 1979, most American hospitals selected white men or white women, and black institutions appointed men almost exclusively. Hospital leaders were trained in business, medicine or law. I am a nurse.

The School of Medicine of the University of Pennsylvania and HUP constitute one of the most prestigious academic medical centers in America. Founded in 1765, the School of Medicine was the first medical school in our nation, and the leader in training doctors through supplementary lectures at patients' bedside. HUP was built specifically for the medical school faculty, which was also a first in the United States. The faculty of the School is medical staff in HUP. When I was appointed to Chief Operating Officer, the School, headed by Dean Stemmler, and the Hospital, led by Mark, both reported to the late Dr. Thomas W. Langfitt, Vice President of Health Affairs. With my appointment, I became a part of this structure.

I had been invited to become Chief Operating Officer, and when I asked Mark for a reason, he said only, "The medical staff wants you to run the hospital; there is not another serious candidate." Almost three years later, Mark commented on my appointment to The Philadelphia Inquirer staff writer Linda Herskowitz, who conducted the interview for a January 12, 1982 article. Mark said, "I would describe her as being bright, thoughtful, decisive, a doer. You don't hit a lot of home runs in a job like this. There's not one major accomplishment; it's a series of accomplishments over a period of years that demonstrates a remarkable capacity to perform well. That's an unusual skill, to deal in a complex environment and to be well supported and respected by the medical faculty. And I happen to know she is."

I began work at HUP in 1959, just five years after Mrs. Rosa Parks refused to give up her seat to a white person on a bus in Montgomery, Alabama, which led to a boycott that bankrupted the bus corporation and began a public fight for racial equality. 1960s America was filled with unrest, including the bombing of a church that killed four girls, the murder of civil rights workers who educated and assisted black people in voting, and blatant kidnappings and killings. Along with these dramatically violent events, some killers merely lay in wait at the homes of civil rights workers to shoot them to death. Riots in Watts, California alone resulted in 34 deaths, 900 people injured, 4,000 arrests and $30 million in property damage. Adding to that chaos, President John F. Kennedy was murdered in 1963 and Dr. Martin Luther King, Jr. was assassinated in 1968.

In the midst of this turmoil, I found myself working at HUP surrounded by white colleagues, some supportive and some not. While I was not physically attacked, I endured such an environment at a cost to my spirit, which was in turn sustained by my faith and by the support I received from my husband and my church. I succeeded at HUP more because of who I am, than because of the atmosphere in which I worked. My inner directions determined what I did, and allowed me to live through these times of racial turmoil in America, while working in a white environment at HUP, with sustained dignity.

John Wanamaker said, "Keep up the old standards,

and day by day raise them higher." For twenty years, this was my practice.

1959

I had applied for a staff nurse position at HUP in 1959, encouraged by Aunt Remelle, my mother's sister. Aunt Remelle told me "HUP was the best place in town to work." She was a registered nurse and ordained minister, a woman of strong faith and a determined spirit. Aunt Remelle had lived in Philadelphia almost her entire adult life, but never had applied to HUP for a position because she believed she would not have been hired. She lived nine blocks from the hospital.

One afternoon, Aunt Remelle and I walked to HUP from her home. As we approached 34th and Spruce Streets, I silently questioned the wisdom of Aunt Remelle's advice. HUP's facilities were expansive, whereas I had only worked in hospitals with one building. We entered HUP and my undaunted Aunt proceeded to the nursing office, asking to see the "person in charge." The person in charge was Julia Talmadge, Assistant Director of Nursing.

Julia, an imposing, tall woman with an authoritative manner greeted and welcomed us. Aunt Remelle told Julia I wanted a job. Without an expression of surprise or emotion, Julia asked if I wanted an interview and proceeded to tell me about HUP. After an interview and tour, Julia told me, "You are overqualified to be a staff nurse, but we do have a head nurse position open." I could feel Aunt Remelle's response before she spoke it. "Charge nurse is right for you," she pronounced as we left the hospital. A few days later I accepted Julia's offer and became the first black head nurse at HUP.

HUP was a new world for me. A short six months before arriving at HUP, my professional practice had only been in hospitals where everyone was black. In HUP in 1959, the professional nursing staff consisted almost entirely of white women, with the exception of Dorothy Clark, Billie Johnson, Lillian Spencer and the late Elsie White. The administrative and nursing leadership and physician staff were also white people, with the exception of Doctors Edward Cooper, James Robinson and Helen O. Dickens. HUP employed a large population of black workers in service departments, all of whom were directed by white men or women. As head nurse, I was suddenly authorized to oversee the practice of white nurses, which was an entirely new experience for me.

Navigating Racism

From the first day I walked onto the Neurology Unit and was met with silence and puzzled looks, I knew HUP was not ready for me. HUP would not quickly change and I could not change. I had to determine how to navigate my way. Racism was not new to me. I grew up sitting in the back of the bus, drinking from water fountains labeled "colored," using public facilities with signs segregating me and those like me from white people. I lived my entire life in black neighborhoods surrounded by people like myself.

I had no idea what to expect at HUP, but did not have to wait very long before it was clear to me that racism was active in this institution. Of those people who did introduce themselves to me, several qualified the introduction with statements like, "Hello. You know, my nanny was black," or "My parents have colored friends," or "Our maid is colored and she eats with us." The people making these comments intended to be welcoming, but did not realize the embedded racism in their remarks. More interesting, none realized that I knew these expressions were racist.

In the corridors and public areas of HUP I was ignored, my greetings refused as people not only did not respond, but turned away from me. On the Neurology Unit, despite all appearances of a professional nurse—cap, pin, narcotic keys and white uniform—my presence was disregarded completely. Perhaps the most egregious offenses were those I experienced in the nurses' locker room, which was space used only by professional nurses. My stockings were removed from the laundry rack on a daily basis, never to be seen again. This act could have prevented me from working, which, so early in my tenure, would have been unacceptable. In time, I came to understand that the removal of my hosiery was an intentional petty act.

Printed notes with racially inflammatory comments were slipped through the door of my locker. I read the notes at first, but soon began to discard them, deciding that the vile language within them could not have a place in my spirit. Equal rights were not on the radar screen at HUP. There was no forum in which to report or discuss these ugly, petty behaviors, even if I had the desire to do so, which I did not.

I made a deliberate decision to move above and beyond the behavior of racism at HUP. I am who I am, and I was determined to do the job of leadership that I had accepted. Racism is an evil that lives in the hearts of people who believe they are superior to human beings different from themselves. This superiority is expressed by acts of self-righteousness, isolation, dismissals and insulting comments motivated by an ignorant spirit. These intentional acts are aimed to demean, devalue or marginalize a black person. Racism mandates practices which can be inhumane and which have the ability to destroy lives, property, and, if internalized, personal spirit.

I refused to be fenced in or judged by racism, even though I always recognized the behavior. Because I am unlikely to seek the approval or praise of others, but rather to march to a drummer unseen, I looked to faith for guidance. Faith led me to an understanding that people whom I could not respect would be placed in my path, but that as a Christian, I was required to deal with them. I did not have a choice but to follow John 15:12, "...love one another, as I have loved you." Loving a person did not mean I condoned or accepted racist behavior; rather, love informed how I responded.

During my supervisory work in HUP, a colleague who I deliberately choose not to name and with whom I shared an office said to me, "The place for colored people is to care for our children." This person was not married, did not have children, and, with her comment, intended to put me in "my place." I did not verbally respond, choosing instead to walk away, not because of an injury to me, but out of recognition of her insecurity, ignorance and jealousy. I was better prepared than this woman; both educationally and through my experiences, and my model of supervising care had captured the attention of others. A scripture came to mind: 1 Peter 2:23, "When they hurled their insults at Him, he did not retaliate."

About seven years after this colleague made her comment to me, I became Chief Operating Officer of HUP. Following my appointment, this same co-worker came to me with an issue that only I, as Chief Operating officer, had the authority to address. As she sat in front of my desk, and made her request (which I granted), I resisted the temptation to ask her where "my place" was.

As I navigated racism, I found that my personal characteristics were a good match for the challenges of an unequal environment. Because I live in my head, I was able to dismiss, and never internalize, the discriminatory behaviors of others. This has, across my life, freed me from entanglement in attitudes and activities that I find disturbing. I have significant courage to walk away from those things which trouble my spirit. Thus, in spite of palpable racism at HUP, I was able to fulfill my professional duties, to change what I could and to not be personally injured. Though my ability to walk away was intellectual, it was my faith that sustained my decisions.

I am disciplined, organized, focused and strong in administration. These characteristics led me to complete a significant volume of work with excellent outcomes, gaining recognition from nursing leadership and physician staff. On the Neurology Unit I was often the only professional nurse on duty. Out of necessity, I taught nursing assistants to do more, which in turn built their confidence and self-esteem. Though I observed looks and smirks from my colleagues, and fully understood their intent, I adapted an attitude of professional aloofness, which offset their hatefulness. Such hatefulness and mean-spirited natures, both common manifestations of racism, are not characteristics of God. I had to address them with God, and I did so in my prayers.

My ability to control my thoughts and reactions granted me focus to lead the Neurology Unit. I set standards of patient care that embraced a medical treatment plan that taught people how to manage an illness or disease. My nursing practice collaborated with the medical plan and set standards to address a patient's economic, social, home and community situations. My goal for nursing care was to send people home prepared to take care of themselves or to assure that a system was in place to care for them.

Booker T. Washington taught those of us educated at Tuskegee through a legacy which states "Let no man drag you down so low as to make you hate him." My early days in HUP taught me how to live out Mr. Washington's instruction. I lived in and with racism in the environment of HUP, but I refused to be dragged down or stoop to its poison.

Two years after I began to work in HUP, I was reassigned to a larger unit, which meant greater responsibility for more people: between 28 and 46 patients, as well as a larger staff to oversee, teach and supervise. This new assignment introduced me to physicians willing to respond to questions about care, and to teach me about their plans for each person. The late Doctors I.S. and Robert Ravdin, Dr. Bill Blumle, and the late Dr. Anna Marie Chirico, among others, befriended and advised me about the historic aspects of HUP's assignment of patients, which enhanced my understanding and knowledge of how to manage care for "private patients." With quiet attentive focus, I continued to raise standards higher on a daily basis, expanding my attention to each individual nurse, staff member, doctor, relative and patient. I modeled with my own conduct the need to push beyond racism, which allowed for an opening of the environment that benefited both those serving and those served.

Dr. Lillian Holland Harvey, Dean of the School of Nursing at Tuskegee, taught us not to be victims, but to use our education, intellect and common sense to build our professional lives. Dr. Harvey instilled in us the need to be personally prepared and not to be deterred by the behavior of others. Her model while I was a student at Tuskegee University served to move me beyond that which was trivial to wholeness as a professional. When we, as students, were not accepted as equals in southern hospitals in the early 1950s, she moved us to a broader cultural and educational experience in northeastern hospitals. This experience reminded me how to proceed in HUP. "God doesn't want us to be shy with His gifts, but bold and loving and sensible." (2 Timothy 1:7 *The Message*) I followed Dr. Harvey's teaching along with the scriptural directives.

In 1963, four years after I arrived at HUP, I was promoted to Nursing Supervisor, which again increased my responsibilities from one unit containing 46 people to seven units, which covered 225 people in all. This promotion required me to call on my preparation in administration, supervision and planning to assure that these patients received excellent services.

The same year I became the first black Administrative Nursing Supervisor, Medger Evers, a Field Secretary for the National Association for the Advancement of Colored People (NAACP) was shot to death in the yard of his Mississippi home. I had not considered my promotions in nursing at HUP a civil rights initiative, but there could be no doubt, I had integrated nursing leadership. Despite the fact that my ascension in the leadership of Nursing at HUP was a result of achievement, there were many who believed these appointments were a part of a larger planned civil rights movement.

I heard more often than I want to remember discussions across levels of HUP that if "the black leaders were eliminated, equal rights" could be stopped. Despite my desire to think otherwise, James and I understood that the misconceptions of others could be a risk to my safety. The growing struggle across America for equal rights caused anger, rage, hate, and expressions of hidden prejudices across races. At HUP, some of the more "intellectual" debate centered on the pros and cons of equal rights, as compared to fairness and justice. I did not join either side as neither had the power, network or authority to bring about the changes needed. I listened and paid attention as America became more explosive. I made a decision that I would help HUP understand what one black woman could do.

Throughout the United States, cities were embattled with racial disturbances and race riots. Buffalo, New Haven, Providence, Wilmington, Cambridge and Cincinnati, among others, were in turmoil. In our own home, we received phone calls at odd hours with annoying comments. I was never threatened, but these calls were harassment. Some people stepped back from me at work. James and I lived in a state of heightened awareness about Edgar, who was eight years old.

In late 1963 I became pregnant, which caused us to realize even more that my safety could not be taken for granted. Then, in November 1963, President John F. Kennedy was murdered, escalating further the sense of turbulence and dissension pervading our country. The persisting phone calls to our home were unsettling in their apparent aim to frighten me. The caller always asked for me specifically, and, once he had me on the phone, would speak unpublishable words. James and I chose not to sound an alarm by confiding in friends or family, nor did we live in fear. Instead, we were deliberate about where we went and with whom, where I ate and who served our food. We paid greater attention to Edgar's travels to school, but tried not to create questions. I cannot say I prayed any more than usual, but I sensed a peaceful presence beside and with me.

We read of horrific acts aimed to stop progress in equal rights. In 1964, for example, in Philadelphia, Mississippi, two white men, Andrew Goodman and Michael Schwerner, and a black man, James Cheney, were kidnapped and shot to death because they were helping black people register to vote and were educating people about civil rights. Each new act of violence helped us accept that my safety had to be on our agenda. The worst part of all of this for me was not being able to walk to work. James determined that he would drive me to and from the hospital each day. He was concerned about my exposure walking at almost the same time, along the same route down 34th Street from HUP to our house, every day. I cannot say I agreed with James; I did not see my presence in HUP the same way he did. But I lived by his wisdom, so I complied.

Nancy was born in the early fall of 1964. I took a leave of absence from work without a specific plan to return. The first two months after Nancy arrived, James, Edgar and I lived in blissful gratitude for this little girl, who became "Precious" to her Dad, and who was adored by her brother who had wanted a sister. As much as I felt grateful for our gifts of this wonderful child and the enjoyment of my family, I because fussy, fat and bored. I spent my days cooking, eating and reading as Nancy, an easy child to take care of, slept. I became intellectually restless. My desire to work rather than become a homemaker caused me mental anguish and conflict until James and I were able to work through my difficulty. We chose not to heed the advice of my parents and his mother, and though they had great difficulty with my need to return to work, I felt that I had to, or I would intellectually starve.

Together James and I accepted responsibilities and developed schedules that would not compromise our children, our relationship, or our ability to manage our home. We determined that Nancy could not be taken out to a sitter or nursery, choosing instead to look for someone we trusted to come into our home.

Our niece Brenda agreed to take care of Nancy during the day and to help me where she could. In early 1965, I returned to the position of Nursing Supervisor relatively free of child care concerns. James, a business owner, had the flexibility to be available to Edgar at the end of the day and on those rare occasions when illness kept Edgar home. At the time we lived in an apartment above James' business, which allowed work and child care to be integrated.

In April, 1968, Dr. Martin Luther King was murdered in Memphis, Tennessee. The sadness of this horrific act was worsened when once again we began to receive harassing phone calls to our home. The coincidence of these two events made me think for a short time that I had been mistaken about returning to work. Nancy was 4 years old and Edgar 13. I pondered what would be the result for my children if someone were to harm me. Telephones did not have caller identification then, and we decided an unlisted number would not do much good. James and I did not know the source of these calls, and decided talking about them with others would generate speculation we preferred not to hear. The callers did not threaten me explicitly, but they were bothersome. By this time we had moved to Baring Street, near James' shop. James worked evenings, which meant that I became anxious every time I heard a police siren near where his business was located. In a short time, however, the calls stopped. We settled into a routine in our home.

Meanwhile, people at HUP seemed to be warming to my position. Colleagues started to act friendlier and were increasingly willing to walk with me in corridors and to acknowledge my greetings. Co-workers no longer seemed embarrassed by nor did they feel a need to explain my presence. My faith grew stronger as I observed change in the behavior of many working around me. I spent my entire days engaged in discussions, supervision and enhancing nursing care. My frequent presence on units led to the development of many relationships which began to expand beyond the work environment.

Looking back over my first ten years in nursing in which I experienced two promotions and survived racism, I see the hand of God. Some people would call these navigations coincidental, intellectually driven, or providence. A hand I could not see directed my life, but still I trusted it. Deep within I know it was God's protection and direction.

Advocate

I don't recall precisely when it was that I met Dr. Arnold S. Relman, then Chairman of the Department of Medicine in the School of Medicine of the University of Pennsylvania, but I do have a clear memory of that first meeting in the corridor of Ravdin 7, a unit designated to provide care to people with medical diagnoses. Dr. Relman, or Bud, as he was called, was standing in the middle of a group of interns, medical students and resident doctors and speaking intensely. I walked toward the group and stood only a short time before Dr. Relman stopped talking, walked over to me and introduced himself, saying, "Join us Mrs. Brisbon." He was inviting me to participate in "rounds"—a ritual in which an attending physician reviewed the work of our house staff. At the time, Dr. Relman was the physician on our medical service who was completing his teaching time. This brief exchange began one of the more effective relationships of my supervisory years in HUP.

Bud invited me to and included me in medical conferences, residents/house staff meetings, and orientation sessions, and he was receptive to my phone calls and visits to his office. I don't remember having a meal with Bud or what we talked about. I do remember that he did not seem to notice my race; he was aware of my femininity, and complimented my appearance appropriately. I enjoyed his brilliant mind and passion for those issues he sought to change.

Bud introduced me to Dr. Renée C. Fox, then Chair of the Department of Sociology and Annenberg Professor of Social Science. Renée is the first woman ever to be named Chair of a department in the University of Pennsylvania. At our first meeting on the stage of Medical Alumni Hall in HUP, where Bud had arranged for us to participate in an orientation for new residents and interns, I was impressed with how Renée's discipline, strong will and persona was so integrated into who she is. Renée and I became friends, and she grew to be a part of our family. James loved her, and my children admired her. Nancy, when she enrolled at the University of Pennsylvania, would be Renée's student.

Renée introduced me to Dr. Harold Bershady, a Professor in the Department of Sociology who became my friend and teacher. To this day, when I pass the International House on Chestnut Street in the University of Pennsylvania community, I am reminded of the many meals I shared with Harold in the dining room there, as he opened my understanding to field observations. He taught me how to study in and use my nursing environment as a learning laboratory.

Many years after Bud introduced me to Renée she told me she knew immediately that I had "the ability to view life from the inside out," and that I was "an astute and talented observer of life fueled by knowledge, social, cultural and psychological understanding in the milieu in which you work bearing fruitful results." Harold, through his friendship, teaching and interest in my future, and Renée, with her friendship, opening of opportunities and teaching, "validated academically" what I knew about myself spiritually. Harold and Renée became my advocates. These two people significantly advanced my career and guided me to new perspectives and opportunities. With Harold and Renée, I came to a greater understanding of my spiritual self and grew more in-depth in faith, which then allowed me to move incrementally in a professional world that was predominantly white without ever losing my heritage or denying the struggles or racism.

By the time Bud Relman left the University of Pennsylvania to become the Editor-in-Chief of The New England Journal of Medicine, he had changed the direction of my health care career through his advocacy. He once joked with Renée about his concern that my studying sociology may take me away from health care. His continuing support and championing of me, however, assured I would remain in health care at a different level. I honor Bud, now an Emeritus Professor of Medicine and Social Medicine at the Harvard Medical School and Editor-in-Chief Emeritus of The New England Journal of Medicine, for his advocacy and friendship. .

As my advocate, Bud influenced my career beyond nursing itself, which in part led Mark Levitan to invite me to work with him in planning. The planning job positioned my advancement to Chief Operating Officer of HUP. My experience as COO in turn prepared me to establish a consultant business born from relationships I formed while leading HUP. It was Bud's advocacy that led the way.

1975

In the spring of 1975, I was invited to a meeting in the office of the late Dr. Thomas W. Langfitt, who was Vice President of the University of Pennsylvania for Health Affairs and Chief of Neurosurgery at HUP. I didn't know him at the time, and approached his Academic Office, located in College Hall just across from the hospital, with curiosity. As I entered a huge, impressive room, Dr. Langfitt greeted me warmly, told me to call him Tom, and introduced me to several men, one of whom was the late Mark S. Levitan. There were others in the room, but the only names I recall are of those of Paul Scholfield, Jeff Stadnick, and Karl Bart, consultants from Chi Systems out of Ann Arbor, Michigan.

I had no idea what the meeting was about, but as we got started, everyone behaved as if I did. As the meeting progressed, it became clear that Mark had been newly appointed to lead HUP and Graduate Hospital. HUP was to be "reshaped" and Graduate divested from the University of Pennsylvania. I did not understand the language used to describe the work. Words like divestiture, capital markets, bond financing, restructure, and legislature approval were not the language of nursing. I struggled to stay focused, remembering my dad's advice, "When you don't know what to say, keep your mouth shut, and don't show yourself a fool." No one seemed to notice that I remained silent. I listened attentively and with interest. I later asked Mark what he thought of me that day. He said, "Bud Relman had told us about you. There was no reason to question."

At the end of the meeting, curious, but still not knowing why I had been included, I went home to dinner with my family. In late June 1975, Mark asked me to visit with him and offered me a position to work with him. I accepted a position titled "Staff to the Executive Director" a few days later.

Some in the Nursing Department saw my acceptance of this new post as a betrayal to our profession. I saw the new job as an opportunity to broaden my scope of services for patients. Shortly after accepting this position, my mother died. It was August 5, 1975. When I returned to work after my mother's funeral, I was less sure about the wisdom of taking on this new role. Mark had previously enrolled me in a program at Georgetown University in Washington, D.C., and while I remained uncertain, Mark encouraged me to follow through, suggesting that I take Nancy with me. I did, and the study produced an entirely new body of information. Later in the fall, James joined me at Chi Systems in Ann Arbor where Paul and Jeff gave me a fast-track course on "how to evaluate and plan a turnaround" of a declining hospital operation.

Challenged by the loss of my mother, a limited knowledge about my new work, studying to keep up and moving my dad to Philadelphia, I had a remarkably unsettled spirit. I worked, prayed, ate very little and struggled to stay balanced. Mark helped me to prepare for the work by enrolling me in special programs in the Massachusetts

Institute of Technology (MIT), Yale University and the American Hospital Association. These advanced courses helped me to conceptualize strategic planning, systems design and project management. Mark personally tutored me in financial management, and had me shadow him in meetings to enhance my learning.

Between the summer of 1975 and the summer of 1976, I engaged in an intense schedule, managing my family, work and studying. I surprised myself with my capacity to stay balanced in the midst of my complex life. My faith grew stronger and I gained perseverance. Oswald Chambers says, "Faith is not a weak and pitiful emotion, but a strong, vigorous confidence built on the assurance of God's love." Perseverance is more than endurance or simply holding on; it is aiming at something not always obvious, an inner stretching until the goal is achieved. This was me.

I was overwhelmed with new knowledge, new people and responsibilities both new and old. And yet, I achieved a measurable goal as I assisted in the divestiture of Graduate Hospital from the University of Pennsylvania. Preparation, faith and perseverance gave me courage and confidence. I was a lone woman amidst a bunch of men, and while I was not challenged by the gender differences, from time to time I did have to remind some men that I was happily and forever married to James Brisbon.

Graduate Hospital

Graduate Hospital was my first assignment in this new work. We were to divest—"spin off"—Graduate to an independent not-for-profit board. I was not well informed about divestiture or Graduate itself, but quickly learned that the operations of this hospital could not survive without a major change. Divestiture had been determined by the University of Pennsylvania as that change.

Founded in 1889 as the Philadelphia Polyclinic and located at 19th and Lombard Streets, Graduate Hospital had a long history in South Philadelphia. In 1916, the University of Pennsylvania established a Graduate School of Medicine at the hospital. Communities value their hospitals, and Graduate was deeply embedded in the culture of South Philadelphia. This community expected the University of Pennsylvania to "fix" the economic decline of Graduate Hospital, but did not want that culture to change. Our "fix" was determined by financial analysis.

Chi Systems consultants Paul Scholfield and Jeff Stadnick determined through their complete financial analysis that the data required a decrease in the largest expense for the hospital: payroll. Thus our "fix" meant that almost half of the hospital's workforce had to be eliminated to stabilize hospital operations. The layoff totaled close to 400 persons. Paul Scholfield and I had to talk to each of these employees and tell them their job was over. There were no options, but when I signed on to participate in the divestiture I had no idea the impact this would have on the lives of so many people. Despite my misgivings, the numbers told me it had to be done. My work as project leader was painful.

We began our separation conferences, which created significant anger, rage and misrepresentation in the community of Graduate Hospital and beyond. I was the subject of talk shows, and the target of accusations based on misinformation. Some people expressed their anger so strongly that Mark and James made sure I never traveled alone on the streets near Graduate Hospital. My disappointment and sadness about the situation were accompanied by frustration. I knew the truth, but did not have a platform from which to respond, nor did my attackers want to listen. Despite this, I held to the truth, and James supported me.

The late James Barber, a Commonwealth of Pennsylvania legislator convened a hearing to examine our methodologies and to challenge the University of Pennsylvania's right to "spin off" Graduate Hospital. This hearing was conducted early evenings in a church on Lombard Street and drew very large crowds. Consultants were called to testify, but I was the main target.

For inner reasons I cannot define, I wore three-inch heels on the day I was scheduled to testify, which meant I stood 6 feet 2 inches tall. I wore a white dress and freshly coiffed hair and went in with my knowledge intact and fueled with spiritual energy. I felt emotionally secure and testified without notes. Members of the panels whose names I can no longer recall seemed satisfied. Mr. Barber was not. He became aggressive, demanding and brutal in his demands that I provide more information. When he could not intimidate me, he became outraged.

I was stunned when Mr. Barber said he was "not satisfied" and that I "had to" give more information. Mr. Barber said, "If you don't answer my questions tomorrow morning, you will be held in contempt." Offended by and disgusted with this man, I replied, "Do what you must, Mr.

Barber, but my answers will be the same." Despite considerable concern and encouragement from Mark, Paul, and the University attorneys to prepare for the next morning, I refused and went home.

Mr. Barber was known in the community as one who got results. During his elections, he attended Monumental Baptist Church, along with a family friend, the late Preston Savage, and my own family.

When I arrived home after testifying at the hearing, I called Mr. Savage and told him of Mr. Barber's threat. Mr. Savage was an astute politician with broad influence among elected officials. I knew there was a "political" relationship between Mr. Savage and Mr. Barber, but I did not know its depth. I also knew Mr. Savage would not be pleased with Mr. Barber's behavior. Mr. Savage told me to "rest well," that he would "take care" of the matter.

The following morning, I arrived at the church not knowing what to expect. Mr. Barber convened the hearing. But I quickly realized that he did so only to end it. My name was never mentioned, nor have I ever known what Mr. Savage said to Mr. Barber. I did learn much later that Mr. Barber had been disappointed that I would not respond to his bidding to save specific jobs, ones in which he had an interest.

My refusal to respond to Mr. Barber had to do with right and wrong. It would have been unfair to decrease the payroll in any way except using the numerical data and hire dates of the workers. We conducted our layoffs on the principle of "last in, first out." I refused to respond to bullying or fear tactics or to compromise my integrity. I had to err on the side of right and would not be intimidated away from this goal. I am comfortable standing alone for right, and, in this situation, I did.

When the divestiture of Graduate Hospital neared completion in late 1976 and early 1977, Mark offered me a choice to become President of Graduate Hospital or to lead a newly established Planning Office at HUP. I was pleased with our work at Graduate but did not feel qualified, nor did I want to manage the operations of Graduate Hospital. Additionally, when a person like me has completely restructured an institution, it is best that someone else guides the healing process that follows this change. I opted to lead the Planning Department at HUP.

My reflections on those years led me to recall John 6:45 (*The Message*), "Anyone who has spent any time at all listening to the Father, really listening and therefore learning, comes to me to be taught...." God had directed and taught me in the course of an extensive study of subjects I had not even recognized just a short time before, and I had successfully navigated their terminology and content. Only I can know the depth of my prayers during the divestiture of Graduate Hospital. My survival was through Divine leadership.

Planning at HUP

I opted to lead the newly established Planning Office for HUP, and Mark placed the responsibility of overseeing and guiding the construction of the Silverstein Building within our department's scope of work. In addition to preparing for the construction of Silverstein, the Planning Office was to develop a program that addressed the hospital's space needs and to integrate the new construction into the existing facilities. We were to plan, evaluate and address the demand for space in a way that would meet the expectations of the Faculty Physicians of the School of Medicine of the University of Pennsylvania.

In order to align ourselves with HUP's mission—to provide clinical services to patients, to teach and to do research—and to meet the promises of our own, we needed to speak with those actually affected by our work. We were to interview the Faculty Medical Staff, professional, technical and service personnel and evaluate what space would be needed. We were charged to determine space requirements by each specific activity; to define the number of people to use the space and how they would do their work; the furniture, equipment and storage needed. Each of the spaces for all hospital activity were to be aligned by relational purpose.

My agenda was full. In addition to my responsibilities at the hospital, my marriage, my teenage daughter, and my son, now in college, were top priority. There was limited time for me to consider failure or to waste energy or time. I had agreed to lead. For 20 years of my work life, I had held leadership positions, all with women. This new planning responsibility called me to lead a male workforce. It was 1975. I was black, working among and in an environment populated by white people. Women in executive hospital leadership were limited and few held this much authority.

Leadership

Iapproached my responsibilities as a leader who hap-pened to be a woman. I cared deeply about the servic-es rendered to patients, which motivated me to enhance spaces, design systems and build an environment that would increase the quality of patient care for our clients and work experiences for our staff. I visualized outcomes and shaped processes to meet my vision. Critical to lead-ership is an ability to build a team of people and then empower or influence them to do the work. Those on the team are required to embrace the mission of the work, and they had to agree to work towards a common vision.

The skills needed to achieve a space program for HUP resided in architects, engineers, building estimators, plan-ners and systems designers. Though I did not personally have any of these skills, I was not intimidated by my own limitations, nor was I concerned about leading men. I like men and my history with my father, husband, brothers, physicians and friends made me comfortable in relation-ships with males. I selected a team of men who could accept working for and collaborating with me. These gentlemen understood that they were hired to develop this program, not to evaluate my gender or race. A few men did seek to undermine my leadership, resulting in their short tenure at the Planning Office. The staff that remained under-stood that while my seat was at the head of the table, I did not work for my own self-interest or power.

In establishing leadership over a staff of twelve men, one female Wharton intern, and two female executive as-sistants, open communication was integral to building a solid foundation. I enjoy people, and, as we worked together, I expressed concern for the staff's families, attended celebrations and funerals, and listened to matters close to their hearts. I found balance between personal concerns and professional expectations and outcomes. Communication and caring enhanced our staff's productivity, as it earned me their trust, respect and loyalty, and helped lead to our success.

Under the tutoring of Bob Geddes of the Geddes, Brecher, Qualls, Cunningham firm (GBQC) and working with James Dill from GBQC, our planning staff developed a "program of requirements." The final project cost $196 million in 1977. As the result of our work, the Founders Building was constructed, the Ravdin, Gates and Dulles Buildings renovated, additional floors were added to Dulles, and the corridor traffic pattern was entirely reoriented.

Challenges to my leadership as a woman were limited, and I have not been sure if there were many because I am black. My spiritual gifts of organization, administration, discernment, wisdom and generosity shaped my perspective such that I saw my leadership position as service work. I am not power driven, but service focused. Because of this, I planned with an idea of how best to benefit patients. My focus on assisting others led me to instruct a construction manager of the Silverstein Building to install windows in the corridor walls of the patient units nearest the Nurses Station. He refused and reported my instruction to Mark, who agreed with my directions. This man's grievance was not with the directive, but rather with a "powerful" woman.

Experience taught me that successful leaders, regardless of gender, require a clear, defined scope of authority. It is crucial that one have clarity about what lies within his or her power, and that one does not accept a position unless or until that designation is clear. I am not likely to be intimidated by men or women when my knowledge is sound, my authority is clear, and my mission is focused. However, while my security as a leader decreased gender difficulties, it did not eliminate them. Some men in 1976 were simply not used to seeing a woman or a black person in a place of power within an Ivy League institution, and such people still voiced their objections.

David Baird, the Director of Purchasing at HUP during the construction of the Silverstein Building, traveled with me to Gary, Indiana to buy patient beds for the units. I cannot remember whether David or I introduced ourselves by position, but the representative from the bed company assumed David was the decision maker. As he talked to us, both his attention and eye contact were focused on David, evidently making his proposal of sale solely to David. Through his behavior, he dismissed me completely.

When David said that in fact I would make the final decision, the representative, recognizing his error and trying to cover his tracks, stated that he "thought" I was the nurse evaluator of the bed. He went on to offer me his Bahamas condo as an apology, an opportunity that I refused. His lack of understanding and ignorance around race caused him to compound his error and place at risk a major purchase. Because my focus was patient care, I still bought the beds, deciding that transcending racial ignorance was necessary to fulfill my mission as a health-care professional. Once again, I would not permit anyone other than myself to decide on or define me.

Balance

I was presented with major challenges in addition to race and gender. As project manager for the divestiture of Graduate Hospital from the University of Pennsylvania, managing criticism and professional jealousy, gaining new knowledge and processes, regulating changes in health care, and developing new relationships could prove daunting.

I could not change my race, gender, family responsibilities or work conditions. Thus my choice was to find balance and to lead or to give up. I never considered the latter. The need to balance multiple schedules as well as diverse and changing activities led me to pay attention to my physical, mental and spiritual health, and to develop routines that helped me and those I served. I rooted my balance in a disciplined daily practice of prayer, reading scriptures and listening in solitude. My discipline focused me mentally, controlled my behavior, decreased stress and allowed me to structure and use time wisely, and also to be available to family.

Friday afternoon concerts, movies or shopping trips freed me from verbal engagement and allowed me to let go of work issues before beginning my weekend with family. I slept late on Saturday mornings where Nancy joined me as James went off to work, and Edgar went about the activities of a young adult. Sundays we attended church to worship.

Holy Scriptures informed me that the body is a "temple of the Spirit." I chose to pay attention to my physical temple with visits to the hairdresser and manicurist, and with attire which presented me with style and dignity. I like perfume, and used scents sparingly. When I arrived at the office on Mondays, I was prepared mentally, spiritually and physically to work.

The Planning Office emerged over four years as a coveted place of service in HUP. Despite this, I refused to be defined by my work, which protected me from becoming possessive, out of balance, and less effective as a leader. Julie Winton describes my influence on her life:

> I worked with Delores in 1975 as a graduate student at Wharton during a summer internship with Mark Levitan. Although assigned to Mark, I spent most of my time with Delores. When I graduated in 1976, I was not particularly interested in hospitals or planning, but I wanted to work with Delores. She was successful at work, had a loving husband and happy, capable children. I went to work for Delores after graduation, a decision I have never regretted.
>
> I used to chuckle when I saw a new HSA staff person in her office spending a day to be oriented by her. She turned adversarial relationships into collaborative ones. Her collaborative approach was a hallmark of how she did business whether with an outside agency or inside HUP with Chairs of Clinical Departments.
>
> We all read "Getting to Yes." She was living it before the book was written. She made sure she understood what others were trying to accomplish and looked for ways to meet their needs without compromising what she needed to achieve.

The most fundamental lesson I learned from Delores is that you have to look at people as a whole—both work and non-work parts. Related is that it is okay for each woman to find her own balance point.

She told me how after Nancy was born she stayed home full time caring for her. After a few months, she realized she needed to be back at work. She returned full time. I had a different experience. I had planned to return to work full time after my baby was born, but she told me I looked miserable and asked if I had considered working part time in order to have more time at home. I replied that I had not considered that; it had not crossed my mind that that would be a possibility."

"That's when she made it clear to me that every woman has to find her own balance point. We each can make our own choice. There is no one right answer. It does not matter what anyone else thinks. We have to do what is right for ourselves. That knowledge was liberating. While flexible work schedules and recognition of work-life balance are common now, it was new territory 30 years ago.

She was very much a woman, a presence inseparable from the work she did. It was an integral part of how she did her work. Her stature (over six feet in heels) contributed to a commanding presence, a brilliant powerhouse. She was stunning, tall, slender and beautiful. Her clothes were elegant and tasteful. Her posture was perfect, carriage graceful and manner gracious. She had long slender fingers with bright red polish and wore slight perfume. She was feminine and proud of it. She not only looked like a feminine woman, she talked like one. There she was, planning space for a huge hospital, and her analogy used to make a point was organizing her kitchen cupboards.

Her ready laugh and charm could be disarming.

She diffused many tense times with a big smile and bright laughter.

She taught me by her example that my role has three parts: 1) to set expectations, 2) to provide tools to employees to do their jobs and 3) to remove barriers to performance. She taught me to expect honesty and integrity; recognize that my attitude would set the tone; to be clear about vision; and to respect employees, praise in public, correct in private.

Lessons she taught me continue to serve me well. Ratings of my department show high employee satisfaction scores, with a favorable rating on every one of the over 20 supervisory training/managerial characteristics. I view these results as a direct reflection of what I learned from Delores.

Julie Winton
Senior Director, Human Resources
University of Pennsylvania Health System

1979

I enjoyed the work in which we were involved and the development of relationships across HUP and the University of Pennsylvania, but my passion to create had begun to decline. I had begun to ask myself what else I might do, whether or not I wanted to accept any of the positions external to HUP for which I had been invited to interview. Working kept me intellectually stimulated, so retirement was not an option. One afternoon in the spring of 1979, I sat on a bench in one of the hallways of HUP, weighing my options as I observed the people passing. We were redesigning corridors in the hospital, and I needed to visualize traffic patterns.

The late Dr. Leonard Miller, Chairman of the Department of Surgery, stopped when he saw me. "What's up Dee?" he said. "Oh! Len, I don't know, I'm weary," I replied. Concerned, Len told me, "Dee, get some rest," and walked away.

The next morning Mark asked me to meet with him. "Delores, are we having a problem?" he asked. Surprised, I asked, "Why?" Mark responded, "Some doctors think you are unhappy and planning to leave." "Would those doctors be Len?" Mark did not acknowledge who "the doctors" were, but told me he did not like the "speculations."

A few weeks later, Mark asked me if I would consider the Administrator job, the title for the Chief Operating Officer. He said the person who currently held the post would be leaving to accept another position. I listened but did not take the conversation seriously. After all, there were others who believed themselves to be more qualified. When I talked with James about the job, he told me to tell Mark I needed authority to fully lead. If I could not have that authority, I should not take the job. Mark asked me to tell him what I wanted—what this authority would look like.

HUP is a complex organization with diverse personalities, politics, professional alignments and power. I could not be successful leading such complexity without the authority to execute the operational policies and practices I deemed necessary to provide services to people who entered HUP. As the operational leader, I knew what had to be done, how to get it done, and who would do the work. Reporting relationships had to be aligned to make appropriate decisions. In the past, reporting relationships had not been clear, which led people on the administrative staff to spend considerable time and effort positioning themselves for alignment or ascensions. I asked for authority to realign the structure and reporting relationships.

I needed everyone salaried by HUP to understand the authority tree and to whom they were accountable. I asked Mark to have my signature on all payroll checks, to have financial control, and to have the power to manage physicians. Doctors determined the revenue streams for HUP. I needed to understand physician practice needs and have the authority to create and implement a support structure to accommodate those needs. The volume of both ambulatory and in-hospital patients coming for service, procedures and diagnostic examinations are the sources of operational revenue. I needed a firm, informed system of control to assure that we earned maximum allowable gains. Systems, support, staff and structural alignment had to be clear and concise with communication to every level of HUP. Having people work with me who could tolerate order, timeliness, and limited delays was necessary.

I recognized and respected Mark's ultimate authority, as he understood I could not agree to anything unsuited for my skills. I don't do well with compromising, and mistakes which can be reasonably avoided are unacceptable to me. I prefer honest disclosure—no hidden agendas. Mark and I developed a trusting relationship, and communication between us was comfortable. We agreed that communications with others were to be understood by both of us. The proximity of our offices would aid this goal. He had offices designed with a common entrance, a conference room, and shared space for Mary Tutt Garrett, an executive assistant working with Mark, and Claire Carr Marucci, working with me. With these conditions settled, I began processes to enhance the environment at HUP both for those serving and for those being served.

1979 – 1986

HUP is akin to a small city. The 700 physicians, resident physicians and interns provided some of the most complicated and advanced care in the world. These physicians practiced every medical and surgical specialty except pediatrics, the care of children. In support of medical practice, we employed about 4,000 people to provide an array of services to assist with delivery of 3,500 babies; give care to 25,000 people in hospital beds; and assist with in excess of 200,000 appointments to people who walked in over a year.

Our employees in this small city provided services in nursing, diagnostic procedures, laboratory studies, radiology examinations, physical/occupational/rehabilitation/respiratory therapies, and filled prescriptions in a pharmacy. Our financial services were organized to collect for services rendered, pay bills, and account for funds, banking and financing. Hotel services included housekeeping, laundry, food service, transportation, facilities, reception and registration.

Healthcare is heavily regulated by local, state and federal governments. I had to assure that we were in compliance with all regulations, including licenses for our services and building, as well as professional staff. Insurances reimbursed the hospital for services rendered to the people we treated, which required us to employ people who could handle these complexities.

The complexity of services required a leadership staff and administrative system to manage the operations. I selected professional leaders with a diverse set of skills to build a team which was competent, compassionate, sensitive and good with people.

Culture

L eaders set the culture for an organization and I wanted the leadership at the hospital to exercise their authority out of a moral imperative, embracing integrity, truth, honesty, courage and compassion, thus creating a culture of caring. HUP did not have a racially diverse leadership. While COO, I hired women and men who represented the diversity of the workforce to serve and lead. Bruce Goldman was one of the earlier people I hired as a member of our leadership team. The late Dr. Maurice Clifford had requested that I see Bruce. We invited him for an interview. He tells the story this way:

> I started passing my resume around Philadelphia to try to get my family back to where I grew up. In the process the late Dr. Maurice Clifford got a copy and passed it along to Delores. One day, out of nowhere, I got a call at my office at the University of Maryland Hospital to see if I was interested in interviewing for a position at the Hospital of the University of Pennsylvania. The position would be reporting to the new chief operating officer, Mrs. Delores Brisbon. I had read about her in Ebony Magazine. It was almost surreal.

I went up to Philadelphia, did not tell my parents, and spent two days being interviewed and evaluated. I had entered organizations before, but this was the first time that I would spend two days and would eventually come back again, twice.

I spent the first morning meeting quite a few people, the most impressive being the late Mark Levitan, who was the CEO. As I look back, he was the first real executive that I had ever met. He was the first person to talk to me about things like market share. The previous people I had known or worked for were administrators. But, I was very anxious to meet this woman, Delores. My introduction to her was to be at a luncheon, after which, I would meet her one on one.

To my amazement, Delores was late. I was thinking to myself, "She must be really something. How else could she be getting away with keeping all of these white folks waiting?"

What was even more amazing was that everyone, including Mark Levitan, her boss, knew why she was late and it did not seem to matter. She was stuck in traffic coming back from getting her fingernails done. A ritual I would come to learn occurred every Thursday morning. I would eventually become one of her chauffeurs. By the way, she went to one of the toughest neighborhoods in South Philly, and was totally oblivious to her surroundings. Being COO of HUP did not cause her to consider a fancier place."

"So, when she did arrive, this reserved, tall, elegant, perfectly dressed woman with fire engine red nails entered the room. Mark introduced her as though she wasn't thirty minutes late. In fact he remarked that we could all start eating now. I was very impressed by the feeling that came over the room when she entered, and I could feel the strength and wisdom that vibrated from her body when she came over and shook my hand and said, "Welcome to

HUP, Bruce, I have been looking forward to meeting you."

When we did sit down one on one, we could both feel it was a match. It was like I was put on this earth for her to teach me what I needed to learn from her.

From that moment, I knew that I wanted to work for her, and I would go on to do so for ten years, both at HUP and Brisbon & Associates.

I would go on to many challenges in my career and in life that I was better prepared for because of her mentoring.

The five most important things that I learned that are important in being responsible for leading organizations are as follows:

• First, when you accept the responsibility of leadership, you must lead or leave.

• Second, you must plan and collaborate with doctors and nurses.

• Third, you must surround yourself with competent staff. To be clear, the definition of competent is a professional whom you can trust, who is willing to learn what they don't know, and who understands that in healthcare, patient and staff well being are impacted by how leaders behave.

• Fourth, you must access expertise outside of those who work for you.

• Fifth, do not let your education get in the way of your common sense.

Delores used strategic planning to set the course for HUP. The strategic planning process allowed the governing body, the medical leadership, and the hospital executives to understand the present environment, evaluate the changes in the industry and focus on the changes and new courses which must be implemented for continued success.

I went on to become the CEO of Harlem Hospital Center in New York City after my days with Delores. That was easily my biggest challenge, and at the same time I had a lot of fun. I never felt more ready for a challenge than when I went to Harlem. The reason was because I had learned so much from Delores. The single biggest reason, as a professional, that I have felt that I could accept the responsibility for leadership are the five lessons learned from "The Great Lady" as she was known at HUP.

Bruce Goldman
President and COO, Health Services
Children of Special Needs
Washington, D.C.

I wanted people to work at HUP as a first choice, and to feel cared about. I shifted the focus of the institution from personnel management to human resources, developing programs for supervisory and job training and counseling, allowing people to voice their concerns and feel heard, and offering market competitive salaries and benefits. I practiced an open door policy to any employee, reserving for myself the right to be the final voice in matters of dismissal.

We communicated expectations in clear, concise, current policies. There were only two policies which if violated led to immediate dismissal without a hearing – stealing or sleeping when scheduled to be working. Confidential counseling was available for people with chemical addictions or to resolve family or personal issues.

While I set expectations for the employees, some were set for me as well. HUP employees wanted more access to me personally. Because of the magnitude of responsibilities, I could not have personal meetings with 4,000 or more people. I conducted open quarterly meetings which I scheduled at hours that accommodated each tour of duty in order to listen to what people had to say. Over a twenty-four hour period each quarter, I listened to 800 or more people. My quarterly meetings created a model of caring and access for employees. Rarely did I need to change a policy or defend a decision. The employees attending these sessions wanted me to listen, and with these meetings it was enough that employees felt cared about.

1983

Four years after I became Chief Operating Officer, Mark left HUP to take another position. He and I had worked closely together for almost nine years. Under his tutorage, I had acquired a totally new body of knowledge and developed new skills and competence as an executive leader. When Mark told me he was leaving, I knew it would be necessary that I leave as well. I had no interest in becoming Chief Executive, and clearly knew there would unlikely be another Mark Levitan.

My working relationship with Mark was akin to a great dance. He taught me steps, and once I learned them, he taught me new ones until we danced together with trust, encouragement, and honesty. In this remarkable relationship, we were friends who cared deeply about what mattered—our families, the environments we navigated, and the outcome of our efforts. Mark was not threatened by competence, disagreements with his views, nor for that matter, strong women. He was married to a strong professional woman and admired her leadership.

I served as Chief Executive and Chief Operating Officer during a search for a new Chief Executive, which validated for me that though my skills fit both positions, my personality best suited that of Chief Operating Officer. I did not submit my name for the search, deciding instead to wait and see who would be selected. During the search, the Chairman of the Hospital's Board asked why I had not entered the search. The late Samuel Ballam did not accept the reasons I gave him, saying instead, "Delores, we want you to meet with the Search Committee." I had great respect and admiration for Mr. Ballam, and complied with his request. When I left the interview, it was clear to me that there was not a match between the defined position and me.

When the Search Committee completed its work, Charles Buck was selected, a person with whom I immediately had a spiritual disconnection. I never knew what Chuck's goal, vision or intent was for HUP, but clearly, it did not include me. He excluded me as he conducted surveys to determine if the operations and relationships among the staff were conducive. While this behavior was acceptable for a new leader, the tactic was aimed to make me leave. Chuck was threatened by me and assigned Daniel Goldberg, the Hospital's attorney, to develop a severance package to offer me. A secretary told one of my associates who informed me. A lawyer in a firm external to HUP called me to say the severance agreement had been reviewed by his office and asked whether I needed him to organize an opposing position in the community. I told this unnamed person no.

Shortly afterward, the late Mr. Samuel Ballam and the late Dr. Thomas Langfitt met with me in Dr. Langfitt's home to ascertain the problems between Chuck and me. I told them about the surveys, his disrespect and intrusions. When our meeting ended, Mr. Ballam told me, "You can work at HUP as long as you wish." Dr. Langfitt and Mr. Ballam, both of whom are deceased, validated my work and assured me of their support. But I had already decided to leave HUP, though I did not voice this decision to the men. My mind was made up. The Chief Executive Officer position and I were not a fit and there was not a job in the University I wanted. Before I could write a resignation letter, Chuck left HUP. I have never known or cared why.

I decided to remain until someone could be named as Chief Executive in the belief that an orderly transition was my responsibility. Dr. Robert Goodman was asked to serve as Chief Executive for an interim. While I had been a participant in recruiting Bob as Chairman of Radiation Therapy, his skills in management were less admirable than his competence as a Radiologist. As I pondered when to submit a resignation letter, Dr. Langfitt left HUP to become President of the PEW Foundation.

A few months went by before we learned that the search for a CEO would be focused on a physician leader. My spiritual voice spoke. "Now." I resigned that day, and left a week later without remorse, sadness or regret. My employment of 28 years had been remarkable. I had assurance from the Chairman of the Board, Sam Ballam, that I could remain as long as I chose. The hospital operations were generating a three percent margin over expenses, the Silverstein Building was occupied, and the Founders Building—a building whose program and design I had led—was under construction. HUP got the first MRI in Philadelphia during my planning and hospital leadership. I had many "home runs," all in partnership with Mark.

Complex organizations like HUP also have complicated personality networks and relationships. This complexity has to be managed in addition to the operational business. I was included in many of the "inner circle" discussions, but found them spiritually conflicting. My personal conflict was not about the ethics of others, but about who I am. After I left HUP, I realized this conflict had robbed me of joy.

Being who I am led me to my success in HUP, and guided me to leave. Aunt Remelle encouraged me to work at HUP. God directed me to leave.

"There is an opportune time to do things, a right time for everything on earth."

Ecclesiastes 3:1 *The Message*

After HUP

I understood that my resignation/retirement from HUP may have seemed impulsive to many, but my decision was deliberate and planned. My thoughts about leaving HUP began to take root when Mark left, but it never occurred to me to seek advice or permission from anyone. Despite frequent interviews and two offers with other organizations, nothing else seemed right, although I knew my time at HUP was done. As Mark Levitan said on January 12, 1982, "You don't hit a lot of home runs" in hospital management positions. I had hit about as many home runs as I was going to hit. I had become restless. My work schedule, public engagement and management of complex personalities had become unattractive. Once I made a decision to leave HUP and walked out of the 21st floor office in the Hilton Hotel, I experienced a freedom I had not known for many years. I felt a cleansing as the schedules were released, and there was no sadness, regret or looking back. I was done. I needed and had a great desire for rest. Psalm 23:2-3 says, "True to your word, you let me catch my breath and send me in the right direction." (*The Message*).

I delayed accepting invitations from colleagues, spent time in solitude, and hours talking with my husband. In solitude I waited for the right direction. I did not want to work right away. In early 1987, I was asked to assist W. Wilson Goode to raise funds for his re-election to Mayor of Philadelphia. From February to May, with Wilson and sometimes David Fineman, I sat in a 15th floor conference room of the Packard building and raised fund to re-elect a Mayor. I traveled to Boston, Massachusetts and Washington, D.C. with Wilson and his wife, Velma, attended wine and cheese parties in Philadelphia and collected checks to record and deposit into Wilson's campaign fund. Wilson was re-elected Mayor. He offered me a position in his cabinet but I declined, knowing I was not a match.

The opportunity to volunteer to help Wilson validated for me why I could not be Chief Executive of HUP. I don't enjoy constant public engagement. I had participated in public events as a part of my work at HUP, through my accessibility to employees and physicians at their will, and

I had conducted myself in such a way as to bring credit to the institution. But, I remained a shy, private person, who prefers small group activity and solitude. Having reached the professional and spiritual maturity to choose an option to be a recluse freed me and allowed me to choose the type of work and the kind of engagement I wanted.

Claire Fagin, then Dean of Nursing, University of Pennsylvania, was the first person with whom I had dinner after a time of reflection. Our conversation during dinner validated my earlier thoughts about becoming a consultant. I had reasoned that when I returned to work, being a consultant would give me the freedom to choose when, for whom and where I would work. In addition, it would be intellectually stimulating, which I knew was necessary for my well-being.

I trusted Claire when she said, "Open a business." In January 1982, The Philadelphia Inquirer published an article on my professional ascension at HUP. Claire, in celebration with me of this article, thought Ebony should do a profile as well. I have never known whether Claire acted on her thought, but Ebony did profile me in a June 1982 edition, "From Head Nurse to Hospital Boss." This Ebony profile led to articles of my HUP work in Essence Magazine in October 1982, and Black Enterprise in July 1983.

I had often thought of beginning a consultant career at age 55; Claire and I had dinner a few weeks before my 54th birthday. Claire suggested I visit with Robert (Bob) Cathcart, then President of Pennsylvania Hospital. I visited Bob who encouraged me to begin a business, but to wait. I accepted Bob's advice and wisdom. He had assisted many of us over our careers, and I viewed him as the "sage" of health care in America.

James and I were celebrating his birthday in June 1987 at lunch in the Fountain Restaurant of The Four Seasons Hotel. Across the room from us I noticed Calvin Bland, President of St. Christopher's Hospital, having lunch with a person unknown to me. Calvin and I acknowledged each other across the room. As he and his guest left the restaurant, this person, unknown to me, came to our table, extended his hand and said, "Hello. I'm Ed Notebaert, the President of Children's Hospital. May I meet with you?" We agreed to meet and at the end of the same day, Ed and I scheduled a meeting that led to the inception of a consultant business. Bob Cathcart had suggested to Ed that he "talk" with me.

Brisbon & Associates

Relationships do matter, and how we respond and treat people has as much to do with achievement as qualifications. After leaving HUP, I established a consultant business built on and sustained by relationships. I called my business Brisbon & Associates, even though the business was me. I did not have an office or a phone number other than our home number, nor did I have a business plan, business cards, brochures or a marketing statement.

Over my career, I responded to and treated people with respect, even though I may not have agreed with them. My relationships have been developed based on mutuality of honesty, truthfulness, engagement and integrity. These characteristics were the founding values of a consultant business that expanded 15 years and provided employment for Edgar, Nancy and Bruce Goldman. Edgar worked with me full time for twelve years and on individual projects for another two years after the business formally closed. Nancy became the Administrator for Brisbon & Associates at the beginning of the business and remained engaged until she entered medical school. Bruce worked with us for several years before becoming President of Harlem Hospital. From time to time, I engaged independent contractors for specific projects.

James was not high on my decision to hire our children. He had considerable concern that employing and supervising Edgar and Nancy would damage my relationship with them and our family bond. Nancy began working with me first, and almost immediately the alignment of our spirits became strength for her growth and my success.

Nancy is a calm, assured, quiet person, which balanced my drive for work and my impatience. Her observations over a day often caused me to reflect upon and alter recommendations to our clients. Because Nancy is more intellectually gifted than I, she grasped that which I was still learning, and could articulate concepts in writing without conversation. Together we became a team. Her sense of order and detail led to the certification and licensing of Brisbon & Associates, management of business activities such as payroll, taxes and insurance. The effectiveness of Nancy's work allowed me to concentrate on client relationships, growing our book of business.

Bruce began working with us when the volume grew beyond our capacity. Edgar is detailed, focused and committed to excellence in his performance, but he inherited my impatience, and needed, from time to time, to be reminded that the clients hired us for advice, not directions. His attention to detail taught me how to discern and pay attention to matters I tended to find boring. Edgar's abilities and willingness to take calculated risks strengthened my decisions, and in one instance, retained a client who would have otherwise left.

Between 1987 and 2004, Brisbon & Associates was privileged to be engaged by the Children's Hospital of Philadelphia; The Medical College of Pennsylvania; Temple University; the Hospitals and Higher Education Authority of Philadelphia, City of Philadelphia; United Hospital, in Newark, New Jersey; District Councils 33 and 47 Municipal Unions; and the William Penn Foundation. Each of these engagements grew out of relationships and referrals. The scope of work across these engagements included restructuring an academic medical center, designing an ambulatory care system, merging hospital operations, restructuring and developing strategies for organizations, advising on programs and facilities for capital financing, and reviews of a variety of applications in order to be positioned for governmental approval. In the course of major engagements, I was afforded the privilege of coaching the executives of some of these organizations.

Relationships

Our first assignment in 1987 began with Ed Notebaert at Children's Hospital on an introduction by Bob Cathcart. Shortly after I began with Ed, earlier relationships in the University of Pennsylvania led Dr. D. Walter Cohen to invite me to manage Medical College of Pennsylvania during the due diligence and merger with Allegheny Health System.

While working in the Medical College of Pennsylvania (MCP), the late Albert Noren came to the hospital accompanied by Donald A. Cramp, whom Al wanted me to meet. Donald was the newly appointed President of the Hospitals and Higher Education Authority. Al and I had engaged in more than one spirited discussion during the time I managed HUP. Al always did the best for his union members, using bantering and good natured discussion with me in attempts to achieve lower hospital rates and discounts. Over time he knew our sessions would end with fair outcomes. This relationship of negotiation between Al and I led him to recommend me to Donald. Donald engaged me to advise and assist with multiple activities in the Hospital Authority, and our relationship grew into a deep friendship extending more than two decades.

My relationships generated three significant clients within four months, followed by the addition of Temple University through a relationship with Patrick Swaggart, then executive vice president. Pat introduced me to Dr. Peter Liacouris, then president, which resulted in an engagement of three or more years, and which led to a friendship with Dr. Leon S. Malmud, who became vice president for health affairs.

Leon and Nancy developed a mentored relationship which led to medical school for Nancy in 1996. In 2001, Leon conferred the Doctorate of Medicine to Nancy as her family sat in the Academy of Music, grateful for how our connections had led to this moment.

While working at Temple, the late Dr. Maurice Clifford engaged us to review and audit the operations of the Philadelphia Nursing Home. When we completed this assignment, Dr. Clifford invited me to advise him on numerous other matters in the department of public health. One of memorable task was the evaluation of health services in the prison detention center. Upon the completion of this project, I realized more about which engagements to accept: those that would not deplete my energy.

Dr. Clifford later encouraged me to accept an engagement with District Council 33, led by the newly elected president, James Sutton. My knowledge of organized labor was limited, but Dr. Clifford told me, "You do not need to know unions—Mr. Sutton needs a health care expert, and the city needs to be sure about that expertise." I met Mr. Sutton at a lunch sponsored by Dr. Clifford in the Union League of Philadelphia beginning an engagement of almost eight years—a highlight of my consulting career.

One Sunday morning as we prepared to go to church, Mr. Sutton called to ask, "Delores can you go to Washington, D.C. on Wednesday?" I said, "Yes, for what?"

Our national union has been asked to comment on the Clinton Health Plan, and I want you to go for us," Mr. Sutton responded. "I need your social security number to give to the FBI. Is there anything I need to know?" Mr. Sutton said. "No, I don't believe there is," I replied.

On Wednesday, with staff from the National Union for Municipal Workers, I participated in a review of the "Clinton Health Plan" in a highly protected area of the

White House complex. While this plan did not become law, the privilege to have been invited and to offer an opinion was an honor and an act of high trust and respect for me by Mr. Sutton and his colleagues.

One of the best decisions I made when I established Brisbon & Associates was to hire my children. For more than ten years we shared offices, meals, work and success on a daily basis. James constantly reminded me of the necessity to keep Momma and Mrs. B separated. Edgar and Nancy were paid based on achievement and responsibilities, provided health care and pension benefits, paid travel for conferences, and evaluations each year. During work hours I was Mrs. B, after five p.m., Mom. Our conflict was limited because expectations were defined and articulated. An added value for Edgar and Nancy was they knew, better than most have the opportunity to, the person for whom they were working. James need not have worried. His family grew closer and remained healthily intact.

As successful as Brisbon & Associates became, providing financial support to our family, access to medical school for Nancy, and later an opportunity for Edgar, I cannot take credit. Our business was proof of Oswald Chamber's comment, "God does not tell us what He will do, He reveals to us who He is." Brisbon & Associates was a gift of God's grace and revelation.

> "You are never to complain of your birth, your training, your employment or hardships: never to fancy that you could be something if only you had a different lot and sphere assigned you.
>
> God understands His own plan and He knows what you want a great deal better than you do.

> The very things that you most deprecate, as fatal
> limitations or observations may be what you want.
>
> What you call hindrances, obstacles, discourage-
> ments are God's opportunities.
>
> Bring down your soul or rather bring it up to re-
> ceive God's will and do His will and do His work in
> your lot, in your sphere, under your cloud of obscu-
> rity, against your temptations, and then you shall find
> that your condition is never opposed to your good,
> but really consistent with it."
>
> Dr. Horace Bushnell (1802-1876)
> Mary W. Tileston's *Daily Strength for Daily Needs*

Volunteering

*"High hearts are never long without hearing some
new call, some distant clarion of God, even in their
dreams; and soon they are observed to break the
camp of ease, and start on some fresh march of
faithful service."* Reverend James Martineau (1805-1900)

I began to volunteer in 1968, when Nancy was four years
old attending an innovative pre-school program, Walnut Center, founded by the late Ruth Bacon and the late
Dorothy Ermish. This program, funded by the School
District of Philadelphia, was housed in a building owned
by the University of Pennsylvania and was located at 40th
and Walnut Streets. The University planned to demolish
the building, a decision opposed by the parents of children
attending the program. We believed that a new location
had potential to destroy the program. I attended a parent-
teacher meeting, spoke out, and was elected President of
the Parent Teachers Association (PTA).

My election to President of the PTA led to negotiation with my employer, the University of Pennsylvania, after the parents of many of these children conducted sit-ins and protests aimed to disrupt activities on the University campus. I organized a movement which led the University and school district to collaborate. The late Dr. Gaylord Harnwell, President of the University, agreed to fund a feasibility study to relocate the Walnut Center. He assigned Frank Betts to work with me. Dr. Harnwell and Dr. Mark Shedd, Superintendent of the Philadelphia School District, reached an agreement which led to building a center for the children on land owned by the School District and jointly funded with the University.

The newly constructed Walnut Center was located at 38th and Filbert Streets, and served four generations before it closed. The auditorium in this building was named the Brisbon-Betts room. This first volunteer leadership success, and the significant publicity around it, led to my volunteer career in forty not-for-profit organizations over a 25-year period.

Many people view volunteer work as "giving back." While I don't disagree with a giving back perspective, I call it simply service—assisting others to meet a purpose. From 1968 to 2010, I have served organizations whose missions were focused on education, advocacy, health services, historical museums, and many whose purpose is fund raising. Volunteering became my work after my retirement from professional service, using the same skills and gifts.

My board service originated out of a need in my child's school, and grew because of my position at HUP and the relationships I had built. I was prepared for board service when Mark Levitan enrolled me in a leadership program which sought to find people to serve. As a result of this training and the size of HUP, I served for seven years on the United Way Executive Committee chairing the Volunteer and Audit Committees. This service built a broad network of associates beyond health care.

The late Dr. Maurice Clifford nominated me to serve on the Board of Trustees of the Community College of Philadelphia. I was appointed to Community College for two terms by the Honorable Edward Rendell and a term by the Honorable John Street. I served thirteen years. While serving at Community College, I met and worked with fellow Board member, the Honorable James Roebuck, a Commonwealth of Pennsylvania representative. Jim nominated me to serve on the Drexel University Board of Trustees, a service I gave for five years.

The late George Longshore, a colleague when I served the University of Pennsylvania, asked me to consider serving the Mercy Health System of South Eastern Pennsylvania. The deciding factor for me to serve Mercy was an opportunity to work with the Sisters of Mercy in advancing a mission to care for the poor. I met Sister Christine McCann and embraced this service because of her, leading to a close relationship with other sisters. During my husband's illness and death, Sr. Mary Ann Basile, Sr. Honora Nicholson, and Sr. Kathleen Keenan, along with Sr. Christine, ministered to my spirit, prayed with and for me, and nurtured me with food and companionship.

When we relocated our home from West Philadelphia to Society Hill, I met Dr. Leah Fitchue, who was at the time a Dean at Palmer Seminary. Dr. Fitchue nominated me for Trusteeship. I accepted membership on the Board of Eastern Baptist Seminary in 1998. In more than a decade of service, I assisted the seminary to merge with Eastern College, which later became Eastern University. My service at Eastern University has used the skills I developed in strategic planning and grew a spiritual relationship with President David Black, Chancellor Chris Hall, and Provost David King, along with fellow Board members, some faculty members, and senior management. Working as a Trustee in this Christian faith community has enriched my life and given me a network of Christian friends, which has allowed me to witness and live out my faith.

Community service through volunteering has given me more than I have contributed. Board service is not using an organization to obtain advantages for friends, or to gain business, prestige or power. Governance is a service to organizational mission, not operational management. Board service is about enhancing a mission through effective governance, advising, mentoring and by strengthening leadership for management, raising money, and representing the organization.

Church

"As you are faithful, this one thing is certain, the Lord will show you great and mighty things you know not now." Stanley Frodsham (1882-1969)

I have volunteered in the church my entire life beginning as a pre-teen singing in the choir, recording for the Sunday School, and advancing to being a junior leader by the time I entered college. As an adult, I have served in three congregational denominations: Baptist, African Methodist Episcopal (AME) and Presbyterian. I engage in church volunteerism as one measure of a grateful heart for that which I have been given, using my spiritual gifts, skills and experiences. Volunteering in the church has been different than volunteering for a non-profit organization and in some instances more difficult to navigate.

At Monumental Church I served on the Board of Trustees at the request of the late Reverend M. M. Peace, Sr. from 1969 to 1986. From 1986 to 1996, I became Chair of the Board of Trustees, based on the majority vote of the congregation. At the time of an election to Chair the Board of Trustees, the Church was in a leadership transition. Rev. Peace had become ill. The Rev. Robert "Bob" Parker was named to serve in the interim and recognized the need to reverse the financial decline of the Monumental Church. Together Bob and I developed a plan to select new Trustees, to guide program development, to improve a financial turnaround, and to prepare for a Pastoral call.

From 1986—1996, I led and taught the members of the Board of Trustees financial and facilities management, acquired a new piano and an organ, and installed a Baptism pool. The new pastor, the Rev. J. Wendell Mapson, through his strong leadership, provided guidance and success in church management and set significant expectations in the congregation.

Despite reasonable turnaround in Monumental Church operations management, our inability to balance revenue with the expected needs became a greater challenge than I deemed comfortable for me. My unwillingness to compromise created conflict and required more of me than I was willing to give. I eliminated conflict by moving out of church leadership, which was a decisive factor for me in my choice to end service at Monumental Baptist Church.

James and I joined Mother Bethel A.M.E. Church located a block from our new home a year after we ended service at Monumental Baptist Church. We did not immediately participate or volunteer in the life of this congregation, but shortly after we did join, Pastor Jeffrey N. Leath, asked me to establish a foundation. I began this work in 1998 and completed the process in 2001. I invited colleagues from my professional life to govern this newly established Mother Bethel Foundation. The late Thomas W. Langfitt; Phoebe A. Haddon, Esquire; Donald A. Cramp, Jr.; Joan N. Stern, Esquire; the Honorable Johnny Butler; David Fineman, Esquire; Sharmaine Matlock Turner; Rev. Norman Hjelm; and Dr. D. Walter Cohen became the founding Board of Directors.

Noel Stanek, a development advisor, assisted with planning, cultivating and raising over one million dollars to restore the bell tower of the historic Mother Bethel Church. The generosity of the Honorable Mayor John Street, along with several individual foundations, the Pennsylvania Historic Society and the federal government contributed to these funds. Shawn Evans, a member of the Atkins, Olshin, Lawson, Bell architects designed the changes and pointed us to funding agencies. Dr. Bernard C. Watson served as our advisor and we enjoyed the financial management expertise of the John Milligan Firm. Delores Bauer administered the Foundation operations.

This massive chore of organizing a Foundation and

raising funds balanced the struggle of my husband's deterioration from Alzheimer's Disease. For James, however, the effort cost him the benefit of pastoral counsel during his final years. Rev. Leath became disenchanted with me and the success of the established Foundation, and chose not to visit James for over a year during his illness. When Rev. Leath made an unannounced, uninvited visit to James on his last day on earth, James dismissed Rev. Leath with a wave of his hand. James' wave of dismissal led to my emotional disconnect with the Reverend, and in a few months to my discontinuing work with the Foundation.

For four months after my husband died, November 12, 2004 until February 2005, I visited other churches. In late winter 2005, I walked into First Presbyterian Church in Philadelphia and found comfort. My colleague and friend, Allen Schimmel, served in First Presbyterian, and invited me to "live out my faith" in this Church.

When I first attended First Presbyterian Church, I had reservations and pause about becoming a part of this largely white congregation. But Suellen Smith made a point to welcome me each Sunday, assuring my comfort. In fact, I joined First Presbyterian because of Suellen. She loved me into this Church. Her expression of love made becoming a part of First Presbyterian a desire. Reverend Jesse Garner ministered to my heart as I grieved my loss of James, offering me a place to heal and to be restored.

The people and the mission of First Presbyterian Church spoke to my spirit, and I joined First Church in October 2005. In May 2006, I was ordained Elder, assigned to Chair the Personnel Committee and later the Christian Education Committee of the Session – the governing body of First Presbyterian Church. My concern about being accepted at First Church because of my race has never materialized.

Some weeks after being ordained Elder, Jesse Garner asked me to assist the Presbytery of Philadelphia to organize its ministries for children. From late 2006 to 2007, working with Reverend Paul Stavrakos and others, we established a separate not-for-profit organization, Presbyterian Community Ministries of Delaware Valley (PC-MDV). Being elected President of this new organization and working with a Board of Directors has provided me a privilege to recruit, work with others, and govern three ministries that serve children with need, one of which is a federally funded Head Start program.

I consider church volunteering to be a high calling, rewarding and fulfilling. My disappointments and challenges in the church have sometimes resulted in establishing higher expectations for others than can be met. Addressing these challenges has taught me lessons of patience, decreased my expectations of the business work of the church and granted me greater focus on spiritual mission.

"The most important aspect of Christianity is not the work we do, but the relationships we maintain and surrounding influences and qualities produced by those relationships. That is all God asks us to give our attention to and it is the one thing that is continually under attack." Oswald Chambers

JAMES AND ME

"Marriage is honorable among all." Hebrews 13:4a

A unt Remelle proclaimed, "He'll make a good husband."

"For who?" I asked.

"For you," she replied.

Our brief exchange while sitting at a window in my aunt's home began a journey that led me to marry James Leroy Brisbon. I thought Aunt Remelle's comment was funny, not serious. I had never seen James prior to Aunt Remelle's comment and didn't think that I would ever meet him.

Aunt Remelle had asked me to sit and talk with her at the window. As we spoke, James walked by, and Aunt Remelle made her "good husband" comment. Aunt Remelle, my mother's sister, had invited me to come see her in Philadelphia, Pennsylvania, while she and I were both visiting my parents in Jacksonville, Florida. I had mentioned to Aunt Remelle that I needed a job, and she replied that, "Philadelphia might be a good place for you to live."

I accepted Aunt Remelle's invitation to come see her. She had lived in Philadelphia almost her entire adult life. Aunt Remelle lived according to her own beat. A registered nurse, she practiced nursing at Einstein Hospital, operated a large rooming house, and conducted a Pentecostal Ministry from her home. Aunt Remelle, thrice married, knowledgeable, and an assured woman, had determined she wanted to share her experience with me.

Aunt Remelle's home, located close to Spring Garden Street on North 33rd Street in West Philadelphia, placed her house near a business owned by James. The proximity of these locations meant that James walked past her house most days of the week. Aunt Remelle's invitation for me to sit with her at the window assured her that I would see James.

Some weeks later, Aunt Remelle asked me to take her shoes to be repaired. I had mentioned to her that I had also broken a heel on one of my favorite pairs of shoes. She told me to "go to the corner of 33rd and Spring Garden, turn right, and there you'll find a shoe repair shop." When I arrived at this shop, there behind the counter stood James Brisbon. He greeted me warmly with, "How are you making out?"

Aunt Remelle had already planned for me to meet James; the shoes provided her the opportunity to set that plan in motion. I soon learned that James and Aunt Remelle had a developed, comfortable relationship. He thought her to be "determined and different," and she believed that he needed a wife. She had told him a great deal about her niece, describing my characteristics as those best suited for him.

James returned our shoes a few days later, and began regular "stop by" visits. These "stop by" visits came at the end of his workday, and did not seem to have purpose.

Though initially he, Aunt Remelle and I would engage in conversations together, gradually the two of us started spending time alone. James and I would sit on the steps of Aunt Remelle's house talking for extended periods of time. He did not seem to be in a hurry to leave, and I enjoyed being with him. Aunt Remelle spent some part of every evening telling me about James' "eligibility" and virtues.

James told me he remained single by choice even though he had had many past relationships and one in particular at the time of our meeting. He said, "I spend time with Margaret, we party and play cards on Saturday nights, and I sleep late on Sundays." He enjoyed being a loner, traveling to college football games and following professional sports, especially football. "I don't like responsibility or clingy women," he told me.

James lived with his mother and sister, along with her three children, on Baring Street, having moved to Philadelphia from Baltimore, Maryland. He and his mother were joint owners of a few properties and enjoyed a very close relationship.

James was an experienced person in the world, intelligent, an excellent conversationalist, and confident without being arrogant. His ability to encourage conversations without judgment or intrusion and his ability to honestly disclose himself impressed me. James had a gentle, yet stubborn, manner that grounded him in his beliefs. I grew progressively comfortable during our visits with his free spirit and relaxed manner.

Several weeks into our friendship, James invited me to a drive-in movie. We shared a foot-long hotdog with mustard and relish and learned neither of us cared much for ketchup. We drank a chocolate and vanilla milkshake. I have no idea what the movie was about. I spent the entire night talking with James. He listened with encouragement and free of judgment, a characteristic which endeared him to me for the entirety of our relationship.

I rented an apartment on Baring Street, almost directly across the street from James' family home. At the time, I rented this apartment to remain close to Aunt Remelle. While I knew James lived on Baring Street, I had not been to his home, nor had he indicated to me where on the street he lived.

James' visits to my apartment became of significant interest to his mother and her next-door neighbor. They watched my comings and goings and the clothes I wore, among other things. When James learned of his mother's interest, he introduced me to his family. His sister Eloise and I clicked immediately; we became friends and developed a relationship that remains intact. Her children, Lee, the late Billy, and Brenda, embraced and became family to me.

Mrs. Brisbon was not pleased when she met me. She let me know both by voice tone and body language that she did not think anything would come of our relationship. James had had other women and the relationships "did not go anywhere." I was never sure what she sensed, because I was not introduced to her as a potential daughter-in-law. Mrs. Brisbon strongly voiced her concern about our differences, emphasizing her beliefs about what would make a suitable wife for her son. She did not like me.

James began to talk about marriage in general shortly

after the introduction to his family, though he did not acknowledge that he was interested in marrying me in particular. Since I had no idea of his intention, I engaged in these conversations, defining the attributes that I would seek if I were to marry. I wanted a person who could support my work, because I liked having money that I had earned myself. The person I married would have to be totally devoted to me, love the church, respect me, and be a good father to our children.

As we continued our conversations about our expectations of marriage, it became clear that our agreements were significantly greater than our differences. Both of us wanted a quality, exclusive relationship and while we had not vocalized the idea of marriage to each other, we spent almost all of our free time together.

Marriage

After a visit to Jacksonville, Florida, to meet my parents, James began to regularly attend church, instead of just dropping me off on Sunday mornings. He made no announcement that he would accompany me; he just appeared one Sunday at my apartment perfectly suited in his shirt and tie and shined shoes. Soon afterward, we had dinner in my apartment, and for no memorable reason, we decided to marry.

We had pre-marital blood studies, secured a license and were married by Reverence Arthur Jones a week later. We did not have romantic music, friends or family, nor had we said to each other, "I love you." We married each other without a formal proposal. This began a relationship that would become a hallmark of our years together.

Home

James had earlier purchased a building at 3511 Haverford Avenue and relocated his business from Spring Garden Street. The building had a five-room apartment on the second and third floors. This became our first home. I worked full-time, and realized quickly that we would need to make decisions about shared responsibilities. Such decisions were not difficult, as each of us accepted the chores best suited to us.

I prepared, served and cleaned up after our meals. We shopped for food and everything else together. James did all the driving, I managed our finances, and housecleaning and laundry became a shared task. We adjusted these duties as my work responsibilities increased.

James and I had starts and stops as we learned to be alone and yet together. Our separate interests sometimes got in the way, but our history of talking reduced stress and intrusions of privacy, and we grew to fully understand each other.

By the end of our first year, James and I had grown closer together, and recognized that giving up old habits provided space to combine our lives in ways acceptable to both of us. We became partners and could say, "I love you." We had made a decision to commit our lives to each other, without a need to make each other over, even as we recognized our different viewpoints and personalities.

I grew to love James more each year and each spring refreshed my admiration for him. He, more mature and self-assured than me, nurtured my love, respected my choices and admired my professional growth. James' life centered around me. While we reared a son, Edgar, and a daughter, Nancy, and maintained a network of friends, we held each other as the highest priority, only second to our relationship with God.

As beautiful and fulfilling as our relationship became, our success must be greatly attributed to James. His strong, grounded spirit, his experience and his wisdom gave me freedom to be who I am. His unwillingness to be influenced by his mother or anyone else regarding me greatly enhanced our relationship.

Living with my grounded husband, however, could be a challenge. His persona, strength and stubbornness challenged my strong desire to have my own way. Our ability to talk, sometimes through the night, allowed us to agree, disagree, compromise or delay decisions to another time. Our willingness to resolve our concerns quickly rather than have them dangle kept our relationship vibrant.

We spent considerable time in our car, the only one we owned. James took me to work and picked me up, unless I chose to walk. One car minimized expenses in our early days, but we later realized that our car travel forced us to pay attention to schedules and provided uninterrupted private conversations. James and I planned, debated, disagreed, compromised and became endeared to each other in our car.

We learned how to pay attention to ourselves in the midst of work, child rearing, church and other relationships. My love for opera and preference for classical instruments differed from James' enjoyment of jazz, but we learned tolerance for each other's choices. We differed in our preferences of reading materials and television, but I learned to read with the sound of the TV so that we could be in the same space. We reared our children in our marriage, but maintained our relationship independent of them.

Children

Our priorities were determined based on the needs of Edgar and Nancy. Born nine years apart, each of them was reared as an only child. James and I prioritized based on their age differences. Our children determined how we spent our time, allocated money, with whom we visited, who could visit us, when we took vacations and where. We did not accept invitations that did not include children, and kept weekend schedules to accommodate church, a fun activity that also taught them social skills. At home we used mealtimes to keep up with Edgar and Nancy's activities. James worked late on Saturdays. On those days we could expect treats, steak sandwiches, candy or other fatty food which we enjoyed together while sitting in bed.

James and I learned together that child rearing required frequent adjustments, disappointments, expense, struggle, joy and extraordinary satisfaction. We agreed about the *what* for Edgar and Nancy, but we each expressed the *how* consistent with our personalities. James approached child rearing relaxed and balanced and I as possessive and possessed.

James reared Edgar and Nancy out of his experience

by telling them stories, by listening and with an ability to guide rather than direct. I reared our children with intense concern about everything—appearance, grades, schools, friends, as well as any other issues I imagined. I feared for their safety, which made me possessive, until I learned I could not always protect them. I tended to lecture even as I encouraged Edgar and Nancy to always tell me the truth. Though we did not have money beyond living expenses, we agreed that college was a necessity. We planned for Edgar and Nancy's college expense by purchasing insurance policies that assured money if our death occurred before Edgar and Nancy reached college age.

Edgar attended a Catholic school in our neighborhood. My heart broke the first time I had to leave him at school. He did not seem concerned, just turned and said, "Bye, Momma." He attended St. Agatha until eighth grade when we enrolled him at Friends Select School. When Edgar enrolled at Friends, we had an opportunity to send him to a camp in Munsee, Pennsylvania, a long drive from Philadelphia. James and Edgar looked forward to these journeys. At Friends, Edgar also chose to play soccer and join the wrestling team. Wrestling terrified me, and I did not want him to do it. Edgar's need to restrict his diet to maintain a desired weight category gave me concern for his health.

James and I struggled about Edgar's decision to wrestle. I acknowledged my fear and ignorance, expecting James to agree. Instead, he said, "Edgar is good. You should go and see him wrestle, learn about the game and ask questions, but stop worrying!"

I wanted to protect Edgar, but James knew Edgar had

to grow and he believed wrestling would also teach him discipline. Importantly, he did not want me to discourage Edgar with my behavior.

Edgar did wrestle, maintaining a place in the 149-pound category and winning many trophies. He gained leadership skills and admiration from teammates and his coach. I learned the game of wrestling, attended matches and provided health services to the team. I lost the fear for Edgar, but never grew to like the sport.

James took pride in Edgar's skill, discipline, and enjoyment of wrestling. He guided me to an understanding of the game, reduced my fear, encouraged Edgar, prevented me from damaging a relationship with my son, and celebrated my ability to change.

While we shared experiences and goals for Edgar, James refused to allow me to restrict our son's growth and exposure to life. James guided me away from fear to learning, trusting and acceptance as Edgar attended late night parties, drove to and from Ohio during college, dated, attended camp several miles away from home, and drove a cab in Philadelphia, among other things. Our ability to talk about my concerns allowed me to participate with my husband in rearing a responsible son. God gave me strength to put Edgar's welfare ahead of my fear.

Edgar got it right as he matured. At the funeral for his Dad, Edgar gave a memorable tribute, but the most memorable statement rings for me: "Because of Dad, all of us will be all right."

My son, born in my early twenties, experienced a young, sometimes overwhelmed mother. Had James not been a balancing force, my insecurities may have prevented Edgar from becoming the self-assured, kind, yet intense, loving adult he is. We successfully reared Edgar and imprinted him with a part of ourselves even as he became his own person.

I gave birth to Nancy after losing two babies to miscarriage. I did everything differently while carrying Nancy than I had done in prior pregnancies. I worked full time and participated in events of interest to me. My uneventful pregnancy turned problematic in the final months. The technology available to assist physicians now was not as common forty or more years ago. Two days before her birth, we were not sure whether or not she would live. This event made us grateful when she arrived and anxious during her early years.

When Nancy reached three years of age, she was accepted at Walnut Center, an innovative program in the public school system of Philadelphia. Our anxiety about her well-being expressed itself. This particular program offered two half-day sessions. Nancy attended the afternoon session, which created a scheduling problem for James and me. Though Nancy spent her mornings with Grandmother Brisbon, Mrs. Brisbon could not take her to the Center and James and I would not trust anyone else. He and I arranged to use our lunchtime to get Nancy to this program. Our back and forth movement to accommodate Nancy's schedule, driven by anxiety, led to a remarkable event.

Our presence in the school at mid-day got the attention of the late Dorothy Ermish and the late Ruth Bacon, the founders of the pre-school program. The program, offered in a building on a site of land owned by the University of Pennsylvania, had become threatened. The University wanted the land for another use. The teachers and parents, many of whom were graduate students at Penn, wanted the school to remain. I got involved in this issue and emerged the leader of our effort to relocate the school and save the program.

When Nancy was a pre-teen, she went to work with me on Saturdays, spending the time amusing herself in the Nursing Office, eating lunch in the hospital snack shop and talking with me. Nancy attended the Philadelphia High School for Girls, a distance from our home, and James and I agreed he would take her to school and bring her home. I had to know Nancy was safely at school, so sending her alone was unacceptable. Only as a senior student did Nancy came home by subway, a decision negotiated with my husband.

Nancy attended the University of Pennsylvania after high school. After graduation from Penn, she joined my newly established business, Brisbon & Associates. Nancy, reared by a poised, mature, confident mother, evolved into a lovingly calm, quiet being, a cherished daughter.

Edgar and Nancy became employees in my newly formed business after my retirement from the University of Pennsylvania. While being my children's employer could be challenging, it did not damage my relationship with them. Edgar challenged me more than Nancy, which was reflective of the mother who reared him. Nancy's calm, assured manner presented limited challenge, also reflective of the woman who reared her. My most valuable contribution to society is my children. Both Edgar and Nancy are effective professionals, loyal, ethical and productive in their work. The opportunity to nurture their growth, guide and teach them is the joy of my life. I like my children for who they are and love them for enriching our lives. During the writing of my story, Nancy and I discussed how she and her brother had been raised. As we reminisced about her and Edgar's experiences growing up, Nancy commented, "It's you. We are the way we are because of you. Daddy selected you because he wanted us to be who we are—you did it."

Edgar once commented to me as I tried to explain a decision, "You don't owe me an apology, you did well by us."

Proverbs 22:6 (NIV) states, "Train up a child in the way he should go, and when he is old, he will not depart from it." Edgar and Nancy, in all their humanness, are "fine adults"—a major joy to my life.

Grandchildren

I have always been grateful that Edgar and Nancy chose to live in Philadelphia and New Jersey. Their decision to live near James and me gave us the gift of nearness and participation in the lives of their children, Emily, Abby and Welton. Our granddaughters, now in their early twenties, grew up within two hours of our home. Welton, our grandson, lives thirty minutes away. Emily and Abby are the daughters of Edgar and his former wife, Ann. Both were born in Philadelphia and lived here until they were pre-teens when Edgar moved his family to New Jersey because of a new job position. Welton, Nancy's son, born one day before my birthday, arrived in this world as I held my daughter in my arms.

James' illness began shortly after Emily's birth and his death came when Welton neared his ninth month of age. Despite this painful occurrence, James enjoyed these children as fully as he could. He looked forward to an annual shopping trip with Emily and Abby at the now closed Strawbridge & Clothier. He and Abby would select several outfits for school as Emily and I did the same. Abby, deliberate and quietly decisive, made selections quickly and then sat with James until Emily made her choices. His interest in the details of Emily and Abby's lives remained even though he could not participate in their achievements. James basked in the presence of Welton. I hold a memory of his frame standing at the crib of this little being, soaking in every aspect of his breathing.

My grandchildren became my teachers. Abby, at age 10, taught me how to use a computer. She wanted me to play a game with her on the computer, but I did not know how. Abby guided me through the game and encouraged me to take a computer course. I did. She continues to teach me to download materials, format and gain greater literacy. Abby chose to attend college in Philadelphia. Her choice afforded me an opportunity to have time with her, observe her maturation, offer wisdom and guidance. Abby and I share a love of reading, often choosing to spend time in a bookstore exploring individual interests in books.

Emily called one Sunday "just to talk." She asked, "What are you doing Grandma?" I replied, "Writing a book." "About Grandpa?" she inquired. I said, "About all of us." Emily forcefully said, "An autobiography is dry, write a memoir. I will send you a book to help you get some ideas."

Emily has a strong social conscious for justice, concern about unfairness, human rights and injustices in our society. Her strength of conviction focuses her thoughts, agenda, and leads her on a road less traveled by peers. Emily's engagement in conversation with me around the issues she chooses to address has informed my opinions and often changed my attitudes. During the writing of my story, Emily graduated from college and is now about addressing her future.

Welton, now six years old, was born as I held his mother in my arms. He spent his first eighteen months with me during the time Nancy worked. This little person attached himself to my heart and healed my sorrow after the death of James. He has grown into a conversant, engaging personality, who looks forward to school, soccer, and karate, among other activities. My bond with Welton is palpable. Nancy calls my home "Welton's Grandma-Land."

Grandchildren are born to be loved and loving. The greatest gift Edgar and Nancy have given me are Emily, Abby, and Welton.

Beyond Our Children

James and I took care of our aging parents together. When his mother became ill, I planned and managed her care. Mrs. Brisbon and I had grown so close that she chose to spend her last hour of life with me. My parents, still living in Florida, needed considerable service as they aged. James traveled to Florida several times a year to assist with the cleaning of my parent's home, to prepare food for them and refresh their spirits. After my mother's death, my dad moved to Philadelphia. When Dad became ill and required a nursing home, James visited him every day, bathed and fed him, cared for his feet and hair, and watched television with him.

I had increasingly demanding positions as my career advanced. When James and I married, I was the Head Nurse at the Hospital of the University of Pennsylvania (HUP). Over the first twenty years of our marriage, I returned to school, moved from Head Nurse to Nursing Supervisor to Director of Planning and Systems, and then became Chief Operating Officer. These advances occurred as I reared our children, participated in community organizations and served the church. My marriage and children ran parallel with my career advancement, but their needs were my highest priority. My position in life required me to shift priorities to accommodate these activities, while keeping focus on James and our children.

Never jealous of other men, James took pride in my ability to manage the diverse activities of family while successfully working with building trades and construction personnel, physicians, architects and executives of hospitals and universities, most of whom were male. His comment, "You were reared to be a housewife and trained to be an executive," assured me of his clarity about and understanding of my multiple activities. James' willingness to support, advocate, encourage and help me enhanced my achievements.

From time to time, James expressed concern about my "giving too much" of myself. I did not agree because I seemed to be able to get it done with his support. He celebrated my habit of coming home to prepare and serve dinner and return to work for late meetings. I viewed this as necessary. Although I sometimes had to, I preferred not to bring work home.. On those occasions where I came home with work I completed it while sitting in bed. My desire to work in bed led us to buy a king-sized mattress to provide space for James, me, and my papers.

Neither James nor I enjoyed surprises and did not spring them on each other. Our decision to shop together gave us opportunities to select for each other while respecting choices and desires. James and I preferred quality items, and our joint shopping eliminated a need to be concerned about overspending.

James expressed his love for me consistently and in special ways. At the end of almost every day he soaked my feet in warm water, rubbing them until I fell asleep. He would arrive with a flower picked on the way home or a bag of Chunky candy bars—my favorite. Importantly, his quiet concern for me calmed and enhanced my spirit.

My love for the church encouraged James' participation. He, Edgar, Nancy and I attended Monumental Church almost every Sunday. The late Reverend M. M. Peace developed a close relationship with James and me. He invited me to become a member of the Board of Trustees and James to join the Board of Deacons. James was ordained Deacon and served 25 years. I served the Board of Trustees for 25 years, ten as chairperson. These responsibilities gave us yet another opportunity to be together, one we cherished.

"But you must continue in the things which you have learned and have been assured of, knowing from

whom you have learned them, and that from child-
hood you have known the Holy Scriptures, which
are able to make you wise for salvation through
faith which is in Christ Jesus." 2 Timothy 3:14-15 (NKJV)

Travel

James and I did not like to be separated at night. As I
advanced in my career, travel became a requirement to
conduct business. Since James had retired, we decided he
would go with me. I did my work and James explored the
city, collecting information which he shared with me over
our evening meals. I am not a person who enjoys sight-
seeing, and this difference in our choices became an asset
as we each did that which best suited who we were.

Our travel for pleasure led us to Bermuda, which became a favored destination. I had great interest in visiting
the land of the Bible—Israel, Greece, and Egypt—and
James had a desire to return to Europe. He had enjoyed his
European experience during service in the United States
Army and had a desire to return. In Europe, we visited
England, Paris, Rome, and Florence. Florence, Italy, gave
us opportunity to share the experience of viewing sculpted
statues of Peter and David of the Holy Scriptures.

We were blessed to have two trips to Israel, the first
trip occurring one month after James was diagnosed with
Alzheimer's Disease. Together for three weeks, James and
I explored, learned and reflected in this sacred land. We
had prepared for our journey by reading the Gospel of
Matthew, which guided us from Bethlehem to Calvary. At
the place that is said to be the tomb of Christ, I began
reflecting upon my journey with Alzheimer's, even as I

denied the diagnosis could be correct. At Hassadah, we viewed the windows representing the twelve tribes of Jacob. I spent time with the leadership of Hassadah and exchanged thoughts with them about hospitals. We traveled to the Dead Sea and Masada, and purchased diamonds in Bethlehem. The Holy Scriptures became real. I read the Scriptures with a new appreciation of the gift given to us by the scribes of the Holy Word.

Our second trip to Israel, two years later, also took us to Egypt. We crossed the Red Sea, the water described in Scriptures to have been divided as Moses and the children of Israel ran from King Pharaoh.

"Then Moses stretched out his hand over the sea; and the Lord caused the sea to go back by a strong east wind all that night, and made the sea into dry land, and the waters were divided." Exodus 14:21 (NKJV)

We went to visit a location in Egypt, described in Holy Scripture as the place where Jesus Christ lived from the time shortly after His birth until the end of Herod's reign:

"...an angel of the Lord appeared to Joseph in a dream, saying, 'Arise, take the young Child and His mother, flee to Egypt, and stay there until I bring you word; for Herod will seek the young Child to destroy Him.' When he arose, he took the young Child and His mother by night and departed for Egypt, and was there until the death of Herod."

Matthew 2:13-15a (NKJV)

We traveled to Greece and took to the sea to trace the journeys of Paul. We traveled to Corinth, Crete, Rhodes, Galatia, Collasse and Ephesus. The epistles of Scripture came alive for us, and strengthened our faith. A highlight of our journey to Greece was an opportunity to stand on the island of Patmos at the place God made revelations to John as recorded in the final book of the New Testament—Revelation.

"I, John, both your brother and companion in the tribulations and kingdom and patience of Jesus Christ, was on the island that is called Patmos."

Revelation 1:9b (NKJV)

I remained grateful that God allowed us to see the land of the Bible before Alzheimer's invaded our lives. God had filled our lives with celebrations, successful careers, child rearing and friendships. We could only wait, as we could not know what lay ahead. We knew simply that James had been diagnosed with Alzheimer's Disease and that our "arranged marriage" had evolved "honorable."

Aunt Remelle arranged our marriage and participated in its success until she went to heaven, two years after James was diagnosed with Alzheimer's Disease. She wanted to make sure that we got it right because she had known all along that he would "make me a good husband."

MY JOURNEY WITH
ALZHEIMER'S DISEASE

Delores F. Brisbon articulates in her journey with the elusive diagnosis of Alzheimer's Disease a realism born of exquisite credentials as a medical professional and blended with 17 years of experience as a devoted caregiver for her husband of over four decades. This hands-on experience is complimented by this author's extraordinary success as a healthcare executive and community leader. Because Delores had been the first black woman in the 130-year history of the Hospital of the University of Pennsylvania to hold the senior position of Chief Operating Officer, she had a large impact upon the teaching of medicine associated with Alzheimer's disease. As a chairperson or member of more than forty community service boards, including universities, a community college, a healthcare system and several other not-for-profit organizations, this author's influence is far reaching.

In tribute to her knowledge and dynamic personality, Mrs. Brisbon was invited with others to Washington, D.C. to participate and personally offer comments on the intended health federal legislation during the Clinton administration. Aside from such professional qualifications that warrant our faith in her counsel, Mrs. Brisbon also earned our trust for she served as a much respected consultant to prominent clients within the field of health care and higher education. In two such instances, this author counseled the president of The Hospital and Higher Education Authority of Philadelphia and the President of Children's Hospital of Philadelphia (recognized as this country's leading children's medical center). This latter category of counselor serves as a model for continued involvement in the outside world by caregivers to patients with Alzheimer's disease. This author's life describes that such a dual focus is possible.

As past President of the Philadelphia Hospitals and Higher Education Authority, the author served as a consultant to my office for almost 20 years. In spite of that close personal relationship, it was three years following the initial diagnosis of her spouse that I first learned of her two-fold responsibilities, that of senior consultant to our organization while also the sole caregiver to her husband, a graceful, yet growing more dependent, Alzheimer's patient. That revelation was a stunning moment; the conversation did not seem possible. Never complaining, no excuses leaned upon, the author's concentration on our business demands did not waiver nor reveal the slightest distraction from the issues at hand. Forever poised, absent of melancholy, her demeanor masked the hurt and reason to possibly become bitter and withdraw from the outside world. Rather, her contributions to society seemed to become more intense, neither as a substitute nor as an escape, but rather from a determination to maintain a balance between her personal and professional obligations.

Such determination inspired her gifted children also to maintain their professional direction and move deliberately in their careers, while preserving their compassion for their father's increasing inability to applaud their adult achievements. They too excelled in their professions and daily living. They maintained that invincible determination to excel while respecting the responsibilities and responses to the special needs of a beloved father, fading from their intellect and grasp. The model of wife, mother, and community leader, while maintaining composure when in the public arena, was adopted by other family members. This capacity to navigate life's challenges, personal and in business, permitted a continued high profile role for the author, while also contributing each day to the public's awareness and need to solve the medical mysteries of this complex diagnosis.

For families and for associations dedicated to Alzheimer's disease, Mrs. Brisbon's memories of Alzheimer's disease will leave a lasting impression. The voice of this caregiver furthers the ability to remain focused, even as flexibility is demanded.

Delores Brisbon, through her devotion and resolve, becomes an inspirational model. May the reading of this extraordinary personal journal help to lessen feelings of despair.

Donald A. Cramp, FACHE
Past President of The Hospitals & Higher
Education Authority of Philadelphia 1987—2004

An Unknown Journey Begins

The most defining elements of my spiritual growt— indeed the transformation of my life—occurred during my 17-year journey with Alzheimer's, the disease that attacked James. I have needed five years to reflect upon our 17-year journey, to grieve the life we lost and the physical loss of James. The lessons of this time transformed me from a doubting believer to a person of genuine faith and acceptance of God's control. I struggled, denied, and tried to hide until God released me and made me who I am in Him. This part of my life could be its own book, as it tells so much about us. But I have decided it must be included as a part of this story—the part that will illuminate all that James knew I could do and be, and what I learned about myself from this tragedy.

My lifelong love of the Scriptures was my real companion during those 17 years; solitude became my friend, pain strengthened me, and the value of relationships and friends reached an extraordinary height. Looking back, I understand more than ever that the control of God is not to be feared but welcomed.

Alzheimer's is a terminal disease which kills the person it inflicts slowly, cell by cell, until almost nothing remains of the original being. Alzheimer's disease killed the personality of my husband and robbed him of the control of his body. When he could fight this disease no longer, he died. I prayed when James was diagnosed with Alzheimer's that he would always remember me. This was a selfish prayer petitioned out of a selfish heart, but my request was granted. Not only did James remember me to the end of life, but his last physical act before he lost consciousness was to extend his arms to embrace me.

Diagnosis

I have never been sure when I first realized James had shifted from forgetfulness to behavior changes. He was stubborn. He would acknowledge when he missed an appointment, but always apologized. I can recall a few occasions when he did not meet a commitment and did not seem upset or apologetic, but exactly when and how much that happened I am not sure. James was healthy and visited his physician every year. He preferred to go to the doctor alone, as did I. We talked to each other about our visits to doctors, and I reviewed written reports from his doctor. There had been no indication of memory related items.

In June 1987, James dropped me off at the airport for a 2 p.m. flight. We planned for him to pick me up when I returned at 9 p.m. He asked me to write the flight number, airline, and time on a card for him. Without very much thought, I did. When I returned to Philadelphia at 9 p.m., James was not at the arrival gate. I was annoyed and tired, and had an uneasy sense about his absence. Nolan Atkinson, our lawyer and friend, was traveling with me and suggested I go the departure gate. I did, and there was James, waiting. When he did not seem to understand why I was upset, my uneasiness became alarm. James always met me at the right time and the right place.

When we arrived at home, it became clear as James and I talked that his thinking was distorted. He was unable to tell me whether he had left the airport, or if he had eaten, and seemed to have no recollection of my writing him a note. The time between 2 p.m. and 9 p.m. remains a black hole. I have never known if he left the airport or not.

The next morning I called James' physician. His doctor had examined him a few months before. As we talked, he told me he had noticed changes in James' memory, but had not been concerned because he had not heard from me. I became irate and demanded he refer James to a neurologist immediately. He made the referral and we visited the neurologist in early July. I also changed his doctor.

Our July visit lasted a full day. James received a detailed physical examination, and we were questioned extensively in order to document a history. James had a Magnetic Resonance Imagery (MRI), and we spent four hours in psychological testing. While James was being tested, I sat in another room alone to complete questionnaires. I cried throughout the process. At the end of the day, the psychologist said to me, "He is a wonderful man, don't worry." We were told it would take a few weeks to collect the data, review it and "try" to determine what was "going on." We were given an appointment to return on August 13, 1987.

I cannot recall being overly concerned about the results of these tests. Edgar and Ann were expecting Abby, our second grandchild, in late August. We were looking forward to a planned three-week trip to Israel to begin on September 2nd, a date chosen so that we could see the baby before leaving.

We returned to see the neurologist as planned to hear the results of the July examination and testing. When we arrived in the examining room, the neurologist greeted us almost too warmly. His uneasiness was obvious. While I noticed his behavior, I did not expect what he said next. Barely looking at me, he faced my husband and said, "It looks like Alzheimer's disease. We cannot be absolutely sure but we think so. I am so sorry." Tears rolled down my face. Feeling as if the air was leaving my body, I was unable to speak. Stunned into numbness, I could only feel profound fear. James, who was stoic, looked at the doctor and said, "Thank you," not yet able to grasp the impact of what we were hearing. We went home in silence.

The next weeks are a blur. Sometime during this period, I got a call from the neurologist to tell me how difficult it had been to give us this diagnosis. He told me he was sending me all the literature he had found, including support group information and social worker contacts. I appreciated the call. I felt as though James's life, the life we had built together, had ended.

I understood the course of neurological diseases—that most, if not all, have no cures, but that many can be managed. In 1987, Alzheimer's was generally understood to be a mental illness that expressed itself by wandering, combativeness, total memory distortion, and sometimes even insanity.

The diagnosis of Alzheimer's in 2010 is more advanced. We now know that there is a list of dementia, but in 1987 the science had not yet advanced, and research funding was limited. After a President of the United States announced he had been diagnosed with Alzheimer's, research has increased and there is now a greater public awareness of this killer. Federal research dollars reached their peak of $658 million in fiscal year 2003.

According to the National Institute of Health, federal funding for research estimated for fiscal year 2007 is as follows:

Cancer—$5.55 billion
HIV/AIDS—$2.90 billion
Cardiovascular—$2.34 billion
Alzheimer's—$643 million

The Alzheimer's Breakthrough Act of 2007 bipartisan legislation introduced in the Senate and House would have almost doubled Alzheimer's research to $1.3 billion. Unfortunately, this vitally needed legislation stayed in Committee and never made it to the Senate floor.

Alzheimer's disease occurs more frequently in the aged population, but is not normal aging. One in every eight persons over 65 years of age, and almost half of those over 85 years of age, has Alzheimer's. Today, 5.2 million people in the United States have Alzheimer's disease. In our Southeastern Pennsylvania region there are more than 294,000 persons with dementia. This disease is also seen in people as young as 34 years old. We began our journey with Alzheimer's two months beyond James' 65th birthday.

In 1987, treatment options with drugs did not exist for James. The first medication for Alzheimer's, tacrine, was introduced in 1993. James' sensitivity to many drugs limited his ability to use the one that did become available. We were devastated and felt cut off from medicine intervention. James was silent about what he felt himself and tremendously concerned about what this meant for me.

Alzheimer's disease is a terminal illness, cruel in its assault on the body. In a brain with Alzheimer's, a protein known as beta-amyloid collects between nerve cells and another protein called tau forms twisted strands or tangles with the nerve cells, disrupting brain function. The changes in my husband depended upon the progression of the destruction, as well as on which cells were being affected. This disease robbed James of himself, took my children's father and my husband, and stole the chance for our grandchildren to know him. I cannot know or imagine what it did to James' spirit, because he never complained. I cannot articulate or describe what happened to the man I loved and married. His spirit remained calm and aware, and he never wandered or became combative.

As if the assault of Alzheimer's disease was not enough, James experienced, over 12 years, three heart events, two of which required hospitalization. He had surgery twice for prostate cancer, struggled with gout and spinal arthritis and suffered two injuries as a result of accidents, one of which required hospitalization.

James and I moved through these periods on a constant path from shock to resignation. I could not understand or accept why God had allowed this disease to attack James. I knew, at least intellectually, that God required an intimate relationship with Him, not merely for us to do good work. I did not understand or accept the third party of Alzheimer's in our relationship.

Prior to James's diagnosis, our life was about as good as it gets. Like any couple, we had the challenges that surround living in a household, raising children, working, serving our community, and remaining connected to our genetic families. But our difficulties never divided our spirits; we were intertwined. This connectivity meant we often had the same thoughts at the same time, and we experienced each other's difficulties and joys even when we may have been physically apart.

James and I were able to collaborate. We were able to disagree without injury, be decisive without defensiveness, stubborn without offensiveness, and nurturing and protective without smothering. Neither of us were given to public display of our emotions, but his quiet, listening manner won him favor from others and admiration from me.

My husband was a deep thinker and keen observer with an extraordinary memory for dates, facts, locations, and directions. He highly valued the relationship with his children, his God, friends, family, and home. He adored me. James was a dignified, strongly opinionated man. An avid sports fan, James loved every sport, but would give up all others for football. He loved reading the Bible, devotional writings, Jet, the Daily News, and any old newspaper, and he enjoyed television. These values, characteristics, and enjoyments were to become friends as he lost himself. Until the last days of his life, he looked at television and held the paper in his hands.

Our relationship served us well as Alzheimer's became the third party and enemy in our marriage. Over our time together, we had agreed on priorities, and our trust of each other made decisions less problematic. We had shared all of our loves for food, clothing, walking, world travel and worship. I am a strong willed, independent, stubborn spirit. James was gifted in the way he managed me. He knew how to enhance my spirit, support my choices, and put me in place when I stepped out. He never put me down. If he had to criticize me, it was constructive. He accepted me for who I am and lifted my wings so I could fly, while he maintained himself. James never boosted his own ego by demeaning others; he remained grounded and secure in a way I have never seen in anyone else.

While Alzheimer's disease was difficult to accept, we were not totally destroyed by it. James' security and ability to accept things as they came strengthened him. My struggle was quite different. I cared for him and loved him more than myself, but anger took over.

My Change

For a time after James was diagnosed, I behaved as if nothing had changed. I continued to operate a business, serve on organizational boards, participate in the work of the church, engage with my children, family and friends, teach Bible class, and tend to seniors in my care. I lived in a state of anger, exhaustion, and deep denial.

In my denial, I forgot how to feel or express pain. I had crushing anger, resentment, and depression, and five years into our Alzheimer's disease journey, I had a transient ischemia attack (T.I.A.)—a stroke. The stroke was small, leaving me a disability that is only discernible when I am exhausted. The stroke, however, got my attention. I had an opportunity to choose to accept that which I could not change, no matter how good our life had been before the diagnosis. I had to accept that doing good works or even that I had been living right did not determine what I had to face. I had to accept that Alzheimer's disease would take James, and I was helpless to reverse that course. I could choose to be angry, deny, scream, and act as if nothing was awry, but Alzheimer's would remain. I could risk my life by hiding, or I could become open to the pain, accept help, and wait.

I behaved as if I were alone. I internalized everything, including the stress of Alzheimer's disease. I did not tell my children how much I was hurting. While I talked to a

A Privileged Life

few friends, the depth of my grief grew deeper and deeper. This period of my life felt like a bottomless black hole—I felt abandoned by God. The pain was so severe that on some days, I could not talk; if I tried, tears came instead. I became protective of where I went based on these emotions. The denial became a physical and mental illness.

In the late months of 1993, my transformation began. In prayerful listening, I received a spiritual nudge to let go. I could not change this journey with Alzheimer's Disease. In my spirit, I was assured I would not be alone.

"His compassion fails not. They are new every morning; great is Your faithfulness."

Lamentations 3:22-23 (NKJV)

I had not stopped reading Scripture, praying, or worshipping during this dark period and feeling of abandonment, but the anger and rage blinded me from hearing, brought doubt to my beliefs, and almost ended my life.

As I released my spirit and returned to God, who had directed me in the past, I came to realize and accept God's control. I heard in my spirit the words of Jeremiah 31:3 (NIV), "I have loved you with an everlasting love." While I did not understand why this disease had come, I had no doubt of God's love. He had not permitted the stroke to cripple or disfigure me, nor to take my intellect. I began a new journey to understanding, to moving on.

"As for God, His way is perfect." 2 Samuel 22:31 (NIV)

I began to hear Edgar and Nancy. I do not remember which one of them said to me, "You are closed," "You are not alone," "He is our Dad." I had become selfish and gone so deeply into myself that I could not hear the two people in the world who loved me the most. I lost my need to be strong and my children became my closest friends and partners in the care of their father.

I learned that strength is not about being able to do everything alone. We are weak when choosing to be closed to help and to struggle alone. I learned the difference between humility and lack of trust, revealing that an unwillingness to trust is a result of fear, an unwillingness to release control, and a denial of reality. I was reminded of 2 Timothy 1:7 (NIV)—"For God has not given us a spirit of fear, but of power and of love and of a sound mind."

Over the years, I have taught others and believed myself that goodness is not the same as an intimate relationship with God. I know that goodness is an outcome of who we are spiritually. When we see good works as our own, they are just good works, not God's divine will. We err when blessings are expected. I was reminded through Holy Scriptures that Jesus was perfect, yet He suffered and died a horrific death. Being good and striving to live right would not protect us from suffering. I had to face our tragedy, but never alone. In solitude, I accepted God's direction, gave Him my spirit, and released James and our future to His control.

I received significant discernment, even peace, as more problems came. I learned more about Alzheimer's disease, and my fears diminished. I included James in this learning process. He had not lost his ability to read, comprehend, listen, or discuss what we heard. During one presentation on this disease, James turned to me and said, "Dee, don't let me look crazy. Keep me together." His request set the bar for his care, protection, and for keeping his dignity intact.

I gained courage and came to an acceptance, albeit a very, very painful one, that James was dying. He would be dying slowly; I would only have notification after the plaque damaged his brain. This realization opened me to every moment and brought a spirit of thankfulness to any victory. The loss from Alzheimer's proceeded slowly. These changes gave me renewed focus. Focus had always been a major attribute for my professional achievements, and I had lost it during my darkness. I became focused on James, almost exclusively, to assure his protection from noise, from confusing situations, and from people who disturbed him with their behavior. My loss of fear replaced with courage also brought pain. I envisioned that we would have to place James in a nursing home or I would not be able to get him to cooperate or he would not know us. My envisioned pain never materialized. He did not need a nursing home. He never wandered, he remained cooperative and knew us until his death.

The Problems

I had to sell James' business; he had begun to leave the door unlocked, lose money and not remember promises to clients. His judgment waned, and distractions placed him at personal risk.

My husband and I had partnered on all decisions, no matter the issue. I made the decision alone to sell his business. I felt disloyal to him; our past partnership had worked like a beautiful and graceful dance, but here I was forced to dance alone. Intellectually, I knew what to do, but the doing was painfully difficult.

James, always useful with his hands, enjoyed and celebrated doing work on our home. Shortly after I sold his business, he attempted to repair a small roof on our house. He set the roof on fire, and severely burned his right shoulder, requiring medical care. Nancy was in the house, and quickly called the fire company. The fire was restricted to one roof with limited cost for repairs.

James recovered from the burns without serious problems. He later broke his arm while washing the exterior windows on the first floor of our house. The windows were some distance from the ground and required the ladder from which he fell. James was hospitalized, and had a pin inserted in his arm. He recovered without major difficulties.

For most of our marriage, we lived in a large Victorian house with tree-lined triple yards. We reared our children in this house: measuring their height on its doors, hosting their birthday parties, and housing the boys from Edgar's wrestling team. Here we had celebrated my parents' 50th anniversary, and shared meals with friends and parties with colleagues. Edgar began as a teenager planting beautiful flowers in the yards every year for Mother's Day. We had never planned to move, but as Alzheimer's decreased James' ability to share in the management of this house, he became intimidated by its size and depressed because he could no longer rake leaves, shovel snow, set out the trash, or "keep Dee safe."

Several pivotal events made the decision for me to sell

our house. We had a visitor one evening, and after James walked him to the door, he forgot to secure the door. I discovered the door unlocked the following morning. We had slept in an unlocked house the entire night.

James grew suspicious of many things. He believed that items had been stolen from our garage. In truth, he had forgotten to push the electrical button that closed the door. These items were stolen because the door had been left open. The unlocked door, suspicious thoughts and two car accidents in which no one was injured made me aware that the disease had advanced. Eight years had passed since the diagnosis of Alzheimer's Disease. I prayed for guidance for weeks with no response.

One night, a smoke detector located high on a wall in our home needed a battery changed. This chore, like many others, had always been completed by James, and when he could no longer do so, Edgar, who now lived in New Jersey, would do it. I got a ladder, changed the battery, and began to descend. About mid-point on the ladder, seemingly from nowhere, my spirit received a message – "sell the house." Alone in the room, nothing else, just this voice in my spirit which I knew to be right. I had no idea how to begin. I considered many options. I did not want to leave the house of our "best" years. I explored the idea of buying or building a smaller house, hiring a full time companion for James, and buying service to maintain the yard. Nothing materialized.

An Answer to Prayer

Several months after the ladder experience, Deborah Willig, an attorney with whom I had worked and who had become a friend, called to say hello. In our phone visit, I mentioned to her I planned to sell the house. Deb suggested we consider a condo, an option I had not considered. She told me "condo living will eliminate all exterior maintenance issues, and provide safety." Her call was not coincidental, but a direct response to my prayers.

Deb recommended Alan Domb, a premier realtor in the condo industry. Jodi Demitre, a seasoned realtor, patiently showed Nancy, James, and me 26 condominiums over three months. I decided on two apartments, both of which were rejected by Edgar for reasons I had not considered. I began to doubt my direction. A week before Good Friday in 1996, we were shown an apartment which was ideal for our needs. On Good Friday, we made an offer to buy, which was accepted within 24 hours.

Our house had been on the market several months, and had received a significant number of visitors, but we had not had a single offer to buy. We closed the sale on the condo in June and moved in August, planning to leave our house empty. A few weeks before moving to our newly purchased condo, a young couple walked up as I was raking leaves from the sidewalk of our house. They told me of their interest in the house, and that they had plans to see the Realtor the following Monday. Without much thought, I showed them the house. After they left, I prayed, please God. By the time we were packed to leave, Mark and Stacey had made an offer, and we completed settlement before Thanksgiving. A process begun in March to buy one home and sell another during a depressed real estate market had been completed in eight months. These business transactions—disconcerting experiences—were a major shift from everything I knew how to do. However, they brought forth a strength I did not know existed in me. I learned that the Isaiah 55:6-8 (NIV) scripture informed my experiences:

"Seek the Lord while He may be found, call upon Him while He is near....Let him return to the Lord, and He will have mercy on him, and to our God,... For My thoughts are not your thoughts, nor are your ways My ways."

We were relocated to our new home, which is within walking distance of shops, markets, banks, post offices, and places to worship. I sold our car, and never had to worry about getting around as public transportation, both bus and rail, was easily accessible. The complexity of these transactions was controlled by God; they could not have been done otherwise.

Caring for Myself

A month after James's diagnosis with Alzheimer's Disease, I opened Brisbon and Associates, a consultant business which we operated the entire 17 years of our journey. Work became an antidote for pain. Serving on the Board of Trustees of Community College of Philadelphia, the Board of Directors of Palmer Seminary, and as a Trustee at Eastern University and Mercy Health System provided me with an opportunity to contribute, to be encouraged, to have fellowship, and social interaction. I had to prepare for meetings both personally and by study. I had to maintain my weekly appointments to my hairdresser and manicurist, take longer walks and eat healthy. The reading and study of Board materials prepared me for meetings, stretched my mind and nurtured my spirit.

Caring for myself through serving others decreased resentment of the limitations imposed by Alzheimer's Disease and diminished the anger about its robbery of my husband. "Peace does not mean to be in a place where there is no noise, trouble or hard work. Peace means to be in the midst of these things and still be calm in my heart." (Author Unknown) Peace bought me comfort, revelations and conviction about God's will in my life. Arriving at a state of peace was not easy or free of pain, but serving others gave me peace and helped me to survive the struggle of Alzheimer's disease. As Thomas A. Kempis (1379-1471) stated, "Keep the peace within yourself then ...bring peace to others."

My acceptance of reality and introspection gave me energy to survive. As I accepted our status for this time and acknowledged my own conflicts, I closed the gates on that which had gone, I grieved the loss of our past and opened space to enjoy that which remained, and I moved toward the future. This freedom allowed for realistic planning to manage care for James, to give to others and to live in thanksgiving. My ability to release resistance helped me to never again put so much stock in my own plans.

The Work

The physical work to manage care for James became increasingly demanding as the Alzheimer's disease progressed. My days began at 5:30 a.m. and ended at 9 or 10 p.m. Over the course of the day, I provided James with personal hygiene, put on his clothes, tied his shoes, prepared his food, and assisted him with eating and dental care. I arranged for him to attend a Seniors' Center daily for exercise. For a time, I picked him up at the end of his program. When this became problematic, I hired James Davis to transport James. Cleanup of spills was constant. Our nights brought fitful sleep. James did not wander, a common symptom of Alzheimer's disease, but he could be wakeful. He would often get out of bed alone, not wanting to awaken me, and fall.

These frequent falls seemed to happen at 2:30 or 3 a.m. James weighed over 200 pounds. Getting him up from the floor challenged my strength, but not once did I need assistance. Directions in how to get him up came in my inner spirit; not once did I need to lift him or even try to.

"Our veiled and terrible guest (troubles) brings for us if we will accept it the boon of fortitude, self-control, sympathy, wisdom and faith. If we reject, then we find in our hand cowardice, weakness, isolation, despair.

If your trouble seems to have in it no other possibility of good, at least set yourself to bear it. Let none of its weight come on other shoulders. Try to carry it so that no one shall even see it. Though your heart be sad within let cheer go out from you to others. Meet them with a kindly presence, considerate words, helpful acts."

Reverend G. S. Merriam (b. 1843-?)

A spiritual routine directed me to establish priorities for James and allowed time to take care of myself and to serve others. Arranging the work to accommodate James' needs decreased my struggle. I had more time to pray, meditate, listen and worship. I learned balance, and gained courage and strength. I was transformed to do what I had to do.

The End

As James' disease advanced, my loss of sleep, fatigue from the work, and the emotional drain from watching my husband die became overwhelming. I cannot define or articulate the pain. I had significant support, and I knew God's love; nevertheless, the journey had become almost too much to bear. James sensed my pain. He constantly asked, "Why can't I die?" I told him it was "God's call." He asked me to place him in a nursing home, even though he had often said, "I want to die at home."

But I could not bring myself to think about a nursing home for him. Then, James contracted pneumonia, which did not respond to antibiotics. His physician wanted to place him in the hospital but he did not want to go and I would not agree to hospitalization. His doctor wanted to see him every other day because she did not wish to give up on him. After two visits to the doctors in three days, I called my doctor, Dr. Aba Barden. She asked, "Are you ready for hospice?" Hospice had not occurred to me, but I knew immediately we had reached a decision.

James and I, along with Edgar, visited the doctor on Wednesday, November 10, 2004, and decided on hospice care. Tearfully, we arranged for the hospice service, and said good-bye to James's doctor. A hospice nurse scheduled for Friday, November 12th, never got to visit. Following our visit to Dr. Gillian Launtenbach, James, more lucid than I had experienced in weeks, took my hand and said, "Thank you for hospice." I was stunned. I asked him what he meant, and he said, "I don't have to take medicine anymore or go to the Center."

Edgar prepared a meal of fish, which James had requested and enjoyed. We later got him to bed. His breathing later became labored. I administered one half the dose of medication ordered by his doctor. He slept the entire night. On Thursday morning, I got him into his chair. He asked to see Lynette Brown-Sow. Lynette came to visit and James then quietly rested until Edgar, Nancy, Abby, and Ann put him to bed. Dorothy and Granville Clark came to assist us. When Dorothy said to James, "I'll see you later," he said, "OK." On Friday, November 12, 2004 at 3:10 a.m. he slept away. God answered James' prayer, and provided us the strength to respond to his desires and needs. He delivered James from a body that was no longer his—Alzheimer's had claimed it.

The Gifts of Alzheimer's

James and I were chosen for the journey with Alzheimer's disease. I don't know why, but God glorified Himself as He provided everything we needed for the journey. Our marriage, children, and resources were available for our spirits and care. James had a gentle spirit, one which did not change as loss came. God was patient and instructive with me, including my rage. As He did for Job of the Old Testament, God granted me endurance. My stroke gave me a chance to listen, change, and receive love. The pain of Alzheimer's disease grew my strength and used my reclusive spirit to handle the loneliness of loss. I was trained as a nurse, knowledgeable about neurological disease and had the experience to plan James' care.

From the day James was diagnosed with Alzheimer's disease, Nolan Atkinson provided friendship, fellowship, and professional advice. He immediately gave his attention to our legal affairs and arranged for a Financial Advisor, Grant Rawdin. Nolan walked with me, steadied my spirit, listened to my struggles, and realistically gave me hope.

Grant Rawdin, from the first day we met in the spring of 1989, remained concerned for and focused on me. When a spouse is diagnosed with Alzheimer's disease, it is critically important to plan for a time when the unaffected spouse may also be unable to make decisions. Grant, with keen sensitivity, kept me calm and focused and moved me through a planning process while caring for my spirit and honoring my dignity, even as he acknowledged my pain. Grant, by his manner, took away my worry about the future while giving me realistic and sensible advice. He is a gift to me.

We were blessed with compassionate physicians: Dr. Donald Schotland, our neurologist; Dr. Seth Braunstein, James' primary care physician; Dr. Alan Wein, our friend and urologist; and in the last four months of James' life,

Dr. Gillian Lautenbach. All were accessible to me in caring to and for James. Through their personal care, these men and woman kept me realistically focused as they cared for James. Dr. Lautenbach remained attentive, patient, and engaged until James's death certificates were completed.

Dr. Aba Barden, my physician, who has always been accessible to me, came for a visit to meet James, and ministered to my spirit as she provided medical care. Her attentiveness to me as a whole person kept me healthy during the darkest days of my journey. It was Dr. Barden who guided me to seek hospice care for James when the time came.

James and I reared magnificent children, Edgar and Nancy. Edgar, a self-employed businessman, had the freedom to take James to doctor's visits, provide physical and emotional care to him, and give me respites. He was possessive in his care to both of us, helping us face difficult choices even as he experienced the loss of his Dad. Edgar strengthened me when Alzheimer's depleted me.

Nancy entered and graduated from medical school during our journey with Alzheimer's disease. Her internship, residency, and fellowship were located a short distance from our home, allowing her daily visits with James. Nancy gave birth to Welton, a joy in James' life, nine months before his death. When it was clear James would die, Nancy suspended her medical practice and moved in with us. She took care of me even as she buried her grief for the man she adored.

Oswald Chambers reminded me in his writings to "watch out for the storms because we are planted through the whirlwind of the storms." Alzheimer's disease was my storm, and it planted me securely, as I accepted tangible gifts of love, care, concern, my children and friends. I could not receive them until I released control and surrendered my spirit to God.

I was chosen for a journey I did not wish to travel, but I could not have my present relationship with God had Alzheimer's not become the third party in my life with James. And so I am thankful, although it took James. My experience with a fatal, tragic disease that my husband suffered began in darkness, rage, and anger. The journey took me through grief, love, joy, and remarkable light. God allowed me to walk through the storm with Alzheimer's disease and care for my husband until the end, and I am thankful.

"If anyone would tell you the shortest surest way to all happiness, and all perfection, he must tell you to make it a rule to yourself to thank and praise God for everything that happens to you. If you thank God for it, you turn it into a blessing. If you could work miracles, you could not do more for yourself than a thankful spirit; for it heals with a Word speaking and turns all that it touches into happiness."

Author Unknown

GRIEF

"Grief itself is a medicine" William Cowper

Cowper's quotation, "Grief itself is medicine" realistically defines grief. The one way to heal requires going through the pain. While most of us are reluctant to grieve, we must. Mourning is not about strength or weakness but love.

First and foremost grief is a process, a journey which requires time. It is unpredictable, uncontrollable and refuses to be ignored. The grief experience is different for each loss and is based on the relationship between the grieving person and the one lost. Grief varies in its intensity and requires time before balance can be achieved. There is no calendar that can determine a date for the process to end.

Grief did not require me to be strong, but receptive, allowing others to help, give and share with me. My receptivity did not violate my privacy—rather, it enhanced healing.

Crying is healthy. I learned there was no need to define, analyze or explain my tears, or to apologize for the intrusion. My crying did for my spirit what an aspirin does for my headache – it stopped the pain, at least for a time.

Talking is therapy. The more I talked, the better I felt. It was not helpful for others to talk to me, but rather for them to listen. Holding written words during grief was difficult for me. It was a year after James' death before I could read and appreciate cards, messages and resolutions. I helped Nancy send letters of thanks almost immediately after the funeral service, but I could not truly engage in the process.

Grief required me to be patient with myself, because grieving took away my energy, not allowing me to move rapidly. Patience afforded me the opportunity to move away from urgency, compulsive actions and unsatisfactory work, which freed me to make better choices.

God understand mourning. Faith does not shield me from suffering, nor does it mean God is not in charge. His presence gave me strength and assured my faith. Church was not necessarily a participant in this faith process. A widow in early grief like myself told me she found it difficult to go to church. She felt that people wanted her to be strong before she could be. She and I agreed silence became the best healer: silence acknowledged our grief without pushing comments that "everything is all right" on us.

I found that mature pastoral counsel from the Sisters of Mercy, an Episcopal Priest and a Presbyterian Pastor provided a significant source of strength. Their guidance helped me to move forward and face a future without James, even as these ministers acknowledged the depth of my grief.

These Christian leaders focused me on the future and gave me hope and expectations to walk on. Expressions of love in word and deed, food and friendship, hugs and touch, listening and laughter are powerful healers. Such manifestations of love may be the highest call of ministry to a grieving heart. It was for mine.

The First Year

I thought I was prepared for James' death. He had been dying slowly cell by cell for seventeen years. I had watched him go from a vibrant supportive partner full of joy and encouragement to a quiet, dependent spirit. He wanted to die, expressing his desire to do so almost weekly. He had said good-bye to many things and seemed to be at peace; he did not struggle. He even made an effort to prepare me, saying, "I am leaving, it's not your time."

While Alzheimer's disease had robbed him of almost everything, he remained capable of making his wishes known until he died. He wanted to stop exercise, medications, and food, and refused to have a new walker. James began to make funeral preparations as early as 2001, shortly after Nancy graduated from medical school. He calmly and clearly gave us details for his funeral service and clothes for burial.

I knew from clinical observations and my long journey with James that his physical life was nearing its end. Despite all of this, I was stunned into shock when he stopped breathing. I was lying in bed with him when his last sounds of life ended. I did not cry, feel overwhelmed or devastated, just empty, and in shock. Nancy and Abby were with me. As Nancy and I stood by his bedside, I looked at James in disbelief.

Kenneth Dupree, a funeral director, arrived soon after we called and took James away. Our friends began to arrive as they were called: Dorothy and Granville Clark, Lynette Brown-Sow, Barbara Ann Joseph, Sean Lincoln. Bret Perkins arrived later in the day. They took charge of planning for James' funeral and calling other friends.

I sat numbly, aware of what they were planning, but not a part of their conversations. I remember thinking James had finally received an answer to his prayer. His soul had gone to heaven, leaving a body which no longer served him. His deep sorrow of not being able to care for himself had ended, and he had entered the arms of his God.

I walked emotionally empty toward the funeral for James. I was relieved for James and sad for me. I was unable to really cry until we entered the funeral home on the day before the funeral service—five days after his death. When the emotion hit me, I had never felt such devastation in my life. I had lost many members of my family and several close friends, but James' death felt as if I had been robbed of a part of myself.

The funeral for James at Mother Bethel A.M.E. Church drew a large audience. I was aware of the crowd, Lynette's orchestration and Kenneth's service, yet it all seemed surreal. The music, Dorothy's tribute, hugs, expressions, and visitations were all heard, but I could not relate to them. Through Edgar's remarks, which I listened to later on a tape the church provided to me, I experienced gratitude for a marvelous son-father relationship. James loved Edgar dearly and he knew how much Edgar loved him. This tribute was astounding—James would have smiled broadly; in fact, I think he did.

When we entered West Laurel Cemetery to inter the body of James in a grave he and I had selected, my soul was overwhelmed with emptiness. I had to force myself to walk, to pay attention. My thoughts moved to how much James would have appreciated the honor guard escort for his casket, the bugle taps, and flag presentation. James had great pride in his service to the United States Army, often celebrating the time he served.

I had to struggle to breathe when the casket was lowered into the grave. Nancy held my hands, and my brother, Welton, wrapped his arms around me. "Don't die," I thought. Aloneness consumed my entire being. I could not speak, I could only stare; James was gone, at peace, and I was alone.

As Reverend Leath announced the benediction, and we began to leave the cemetery, my personality seemed to split—a part of me wanted to stay, and another part said to go. In the end, I walked to the waiting car, certain that no one could be aware of my desire to die, which seemed to be easier than living.

We gathered at the Downtown Club for food. I had absolutely no interest in eating, but felt compelled to attend the event. I felt irritable and wanted to get out. Bret Perkins and Payne Brown walked over to me, and, upon my request, walked with me to my home. There Bret and Payne sat with me, drew me into conversation, and opened me to loss as they helped me celebrate the success of my marriage. I was shocked by my feelings of irritability as I acknowledged widowhood. I no longer had the physical presence of a significant part of myself. Sorrow crushed my spirit. I felt God's presence but could only lean on it; I had no strength of my own.

In the immediate weeks after James' burial, I could not focus. My heart refused to cooperate with my head. Some days, this separation made me feel on the edge of insanity. My memory was terrible, and when I realized this, I became frightened. Sometimes James seemed to be floating above me, just out of reach for me to touch. This visual sensation confused me. I could not read with comprehension, because I could not remember what I read. I was grateful for scriptures already in my spirit as I felt the presence of God in spite of the confusion of my mind.

Eating was a chore—food, no matter how well prepared or presented, held no interest for me. I could not sleep, a pattern established during James' illness. Now my insomnia was driven by a desire not to sleep—I was trying to remember. I lived for weeks in a state of exhaustion and drowsiness. It seemed my tears had no end. They came without control in public or private. I cried whenever I saw a man wearing a cap and leaning on a cane, or couples holding hands in the park. When I attempted to hold my tears back, it made me physically ill. I had to cry so that I could breathe. Depression became my companion.

I suffered periods of tremendous guilt for all sorts of things. I questioned and analyzed all my decisions regarding James' care. My spirit was filled with anxiety, doubt, and anger. Intellectually and spiritually, I knew my thoughts were without merit, but this did not seem to matter. I became self-centered and self-absorbed. I talked about James non-stop to anyone who listened. My conversations and thoughts were consumed with James, his last words and actions. Some of these things may have been distorted by my grief, but they were true to me at the time.

Because James died in November, Thanksgiving came two weeks after his death, followed by our wedding anniversary in early December, then the Christmas holidays. These milestones were especially difficult. I spent December in physical and emotional pain. Almost six years later, I am unable to describe the varying levels of distress, loss, and deep sorrow.

In the first months, I did not find church attendance helpful. Many people did not seem to understand that grief is not shielded by faith. I could not accept nor did I want to hear that James was "better off," "out of pain," "in heaven." While these comments were well meaning, they were useless. Those speaking these words did not understand my loss, or that grief is painful regardless of a faith in God and a belief of heaven. I began to visit churches where I was not known.

Comfort

The second Beatitude recorded in Matthew 5:4 (NIV) of the New Testament states, "Blessed are those who mourn, for they will be comforted." As I mourned the loss of James, I was comforted in very many ways, especially by my grandson.

I missed the work of James' care, and found myself looking for something to fill the tremendous void. The daytime was less difficult because I was caring for Welton, nine months old and beginning to show curiosity in everything around him. Welton comforted me. He sensed my sorrow, expressing love by rubbing my face as I cried. Welton's presence kept me focused on moving forward. His care required me to take him outside, and, with him in a stroller, we walked long distances almost every day. Upon returning, we would take extended naps in the afternoon. These activities provided exercise and rest for me during the daytime, initiating deep healing.

Welton's awareness of things around him gave me opportunities to explore ways to enhance his development. We became fully engaged in reading, listening to Mozart, and just being, which provided a significant comfort.

Comfort also came from many people through their acts of kindness. In the early days, Dorothy and Granville Clark provided companionship and food, attended church with me, called daily and gave attention to my health. The late Madeline Ballard provided food, interest in and responses to anything I spoke of or mentioned. Bret and Donna Perkins were intentional in seeing that I got out, taking me to dinner, movies, and concerts. Everyone expressed love without intruding into my privacy.

In January, three months after James died, the fatigue that had been brought on by the months of care and emotional pain required me to take a respite. I decided to go to Bermuda, a place James and I had enjoyed over the course of our travel days. Lynette Brown-Sow volunteered to go with me. During this trip, Lynette skillfully gave me time alone without leaving me lonely. While Lynette and I sat on a veranda in Bermuda, I told her "my condo seemed foreign for me." She said, "Let's rearrange the rooms, something I have wanted to do for a long time." Her calm and skillful planning led to a rearrangement that enhanced the beauty of my home and made it comfortable for me.

Payne Brown helped me to release my guilt with one telephone call. In the first months he called at least twice a week. In one such call, I told Payne of my feelings of guilt. Without missing a beat, Payne told me, "The problem is not guilt, Mrs. Brisbon. Mr. Brisbon wanted to go and you wanted him to stay. There is no reason for you to be guilty." Payne's comments made me recognize that my feelings were not of guilt, but anger because I could not control an outcome. I realized instantaneously, once again, that God was in control. He alone decided whether James lived or died. Payne's comments brought me astounding comfort.

Mary Garrett's words of comfort were powerful for me as well. While telling her about my visual sensation of James floating above me, Mary commented, "He is ascending. When you can let him go, his earthly journey will be done." These words freed me to accept what I already believed.

Sleep did not come easily for many months, but in the brief time it did, my dreams were filled with light. My dreams seemed to place me in another world. I felt loved and nurtured, surrounded by a presence; there were no voice or faces, just presence and light. When I would awake, comfort and serenity dominated my emotions.

The gifts of comfort came in all forms: meals, candles, cash, visits, invitations, and flowers. These acts of kindness extended well into the six months after James' funeral. Over 50 persons made gifts in James' memory to the Alzheimer's Association.

Pastoral counsel was a major source of comfort. My

support came from pastors and persons not associated with my denomination. At the time of James' death, I was an African Methodist Episcopal congregant, but my support came from an Episcopalian Rector, the Sisters of Mercy, and a Presbyterian Pastor. The Sisters of Mercy extended themselves to me in tenderness, love, and understanding. Sister Christine McCann and Sister Mary Ann Basile in particular, kept in close contact, supporting me through periods of tears, providing readings, talking with me, and engaging in prayer for me. The Reverend Rodger Broadly, the Rector of Saint Luke of the Epiphany Episcopal Church and Nancy's pastor, visited and counseled me, encouraging me to "walk on." His words remain a source of hope. Rodger told me "You walked as far as you could with James, now you must walk on." On days when walking on seemed impossible, Rodger's words gave me the hope and strength to move forward. He encouraged me to write and now I am.

During the very dark few months immediately following James' death, I searched my spirit, trying to determine if I needed any church membership. I walked into First Presbyterian Church in Philadelphia in February 2005 and my life began to receive light. Reverend Jesse Garner reached out to me, and came to my home to visit. In our conversation, he acknowledged the pain of my grief, but focused my thoughts on the future, as he offered support for the present. During our visit, Jesse offered me personal counsel and support in moving forward, as well as the service of the church as a place to rest and heal. His acceptance of me, his persona and attitude, coupled with loving concern, ministered to my grieving heart, expecting nothing in return except my healing. His support to me left me truly comforted.

The comfort provided to me from those God placed in my life moved me forward. Eleven months after James' death, I began to get through a day without tears. I began to concentrate on something other than myself and I started responding to a call to participate in life again. In early November 2005, I was attacked with a sorrow that collapsed me to weakness, tears, and despair. The attack came without warning, but the emotional response was cleansing. My tears washed something out. While sorrow and sadness remained, significant peace filled other spaces. God had bought me to the end of the first year. My mind began to focus. I accepted that the depth of my grief was reflective of the depth of my love. Had I not loved James deeply, the grief would have been different. Grief will always be a part of me—it is my heart's memorial, a gift for the years we shared and loved. James will always be a part of me in my spirit. Death cannot take him away.

> *"When we asunder part*
> *It gives us inward pain*
> *But we are joined in heart*
> *And hope to meet again."*
>
> Fawcett—May 28, 2007, Daily Word

On November 12, 2005, the first anniversary of James's death, I acknowledged publicly that I had survived the year. While grief had not ended, the time had come to say thank you to 30 special friends, each of whom could claim responsibility for my year of healing, growing, accepting, and beginning to move forward.

We gathered in the Chairman's Room of Davio's Restaurant for lunch. It seemed right to acknowledge others in one of James' favorite places. Peter Jolly, its owner, had planned more than one birthday meal for James and we often ate dinner with our children at this restaurant. We enjoyed food, laughter, fellowship, and memories. I could smile again, one weight of grieving lifted. I know in my spirit that James was pleased.

We invited friends to write memories of James. Edgar captured these notes in a book "Remembering James L. Brisbon." I honored James' memory with my memorial to him. I remember:

- Witness as a Christian as you face the challenges of your life
- Our conversations in the car
- Encouragement during my challenges
- Encouragement to be the best I could be
- Embraces to put me to sleep during extreme exhaustion
- Encouragement to let our children grow
- Stubbornness
- Excitement of the birth of our grandchildren
- Being my best friend

As I walked on, Tom Petro, a colleague at Eastern University where we serve on the Board of Trustees, invited me to dinner. Tom ministered to my spirit even though it had begun to heal and I had begun to "walk on." As we shared mutual spiritual experiences, Tom said, "God always brings light after darkness." His comment highlighted for me that my grief had reached another level—God had provided the light.

God had given me the accessibility and availability to "walk on" emerged in light. I embraced grief as it spoke; I opened my spirit, healed, and became transformed. I can love again, if God chooses. Indeed, "grief is medicine"; I received the medicine and began to heal. I have no idea if I will ever be "cured," but the treatment provided by God assures me that He will be with me. God has healed me to give to others.

"The Father of mercies and God of all comfort who comforts us in tribulation that we may be able to comfort those who are in any trouble with the comfort with which we ourselves are comforted."

2 Corinthians 1:3-4 (NKJV)

LESSONS FROM LIFE

"An open mind collects more riches than an open purse." Author Unknown

These lessons, learned over the seven decades of my life, have served me abundantly.

1. **Believe in a Power greater than your own.** For me, the power of God is greater than any other power. This belief has guided me to carry out that which I can do with expectations of an outcome bigger than myself and the trust of excellence. Believing in the God I cannot see, explain or understand does not concern me, because my spiritual relationship, maintained through prayer and Holy Scriptures, has given me contentment. For anyone who does not believe in God, look for something bigger than oneself, because personal views can be too narrow to see the horizons of possibility.

2. **Be who you are.** I have lived and celebrated the unique human being I am made to be, free and authentic, which has given me a security that diminishes comparisons with others, even as I respect their humanity. Within yourself be in touch with your charac-

ter and this will focus your decisions, relationships and choices. Being true to who you are removes unrealistic desires, needs and struggles.

3. **Change occurs** when participants in a situation or relationship determine that a different direction or perspective is needed. My lesson has been a recognition that I may influence change for others, but I can only make an actual change in myself.

4. **Failure, mistakes, incorrect assumptions,** can be the beginning of growth and newness once the pain diminishes. My growth has come when I have recognized failures born out of my selfishness.

5. **Suffering teaches perseverance,** stretches intellect, tests emotions, opens the heart and increases an ability to see. Embracing suffering pushed me so low, I had to look up to live.

6. **Love is a verb,** something to be done. I learned that when love has been my motivation, whatever the outcome, all is well.

7. **Relationships are foundational** to mental and spiritual well-being. When based on trust and honesty, lack of inappropriate control and open communication, they will survive storms. Relationships, like a garden of flowers, can have many varieties of beauty. Some are harder to grow than others, but with cultivation they can come to full maturity, blooming with respect and companionship. I learned that all relationships require work, but that not all are meant to last. Some will and must end.

8. **Marriage requires love and unselfishness,** tolerance and patience, forgiveness and release, adjust-

ment and change, much of which is painful, but the result is joy—an inner spirit emotion.

9. **Grandchildren are to be loved.**

10. **Mentoring is a precious gift,** both when received from others and when given to those needing help.

11. **Listening allows others to speak** and helps them clarify their thoughts, deepen their thinking, and claim their desires. Body language also has a voice. I learned to listen with my heart and eyes, as well as my ears, picking up information that conveyed to me a deeper meaning than words alone.

12. **Solitude is a walk in a quiet wilderness** from darkness to light. In solitude I have learned how to recognize my mistakes, confess spiritually to wrongs, release guilt, and give up **my** way in order to gain clarity. During times of solitude I have been guided to determine what I will speak and what I will do.

13. **Prayer—Scripture has told me to pray without ceasing.** I can pray anywhere about anything and everybody because prayer is like breathing to me.

QUOTATIONS BY CHAPTER

Scriptures quoted below are from:

The New International Version (NIV) – 11 verses

The Message – 5 verses

New King James Version (NKJV) – 6 verses

Copyright laws allow up to 500 verses from any one source.

Chapter	Quote	Source	Page
Intro.	Psalm 139:15	*The Message*	v
	Samuel D. Robbins		xi
My Beginnings			
	Proverbs 3:5,6	*NIV*	1
	Jeremiah 29:11	*NIV*	15
	2002 Tuskegee Alumni Directory		16
	Booker T. Washington		22
	Proverbs 3:7A	*NIV*	26
Work in Philadelphia			
	**Oswald Chambers		27
	Philadelphia Inquirer – January 12, 1982		28
	*John Wanamaker	Tileston	29
	John 15:12	*NIV*	33
	1 Peter 2:23	*NIV*	34
	*Booker T. Washington		35
	2 Timothy 1:7	*The Message*	36
	**Oswald Chambers		46
	John 6:45	*The Message*	50
	Ecclesiastes 3:1	*The Message*	70
	Psalm 23:2-3	*The Message*	71

*Horace Bushnell	Tileston	77
*James Martineau	Tileston	79
*Stanley Frodsham	Tileston	82
**Oswald Chambers		86

James and Me

Hebrews 13:4a	*NIV*	87
Proverbs 22:6	*NIV*	99
2 Timothy 13:14-15	*NKJV*	103
Exodus 14:21	*NKJV*	105
Matthew 2:13-15	*NKJV*	105
Revelation 1:9b	*NKJV*	106

My Journey with Alzheimer's Disease

Lamentations 3:22-23	NKJV	118
Jeremiah 31:3	NIV	119
2 Samuel 22:31	NIV	119
2 Timothy 1:7	NIV	119
Isaiah 55:6-8	NIV	124
Unknown Author		125
*Thomas A. Kempus	Tileston	126
*G. S. Merriam	Tileston	127
Unknown Author		132

Grief

William Cowper		133
Matthew 5:4	NIV	139
Fawcett	Daily Word, May 28, 2007	143
2 Corinthians 1:3-4	NKJV	145

*Tileston's "Daily Strength for Daily Needs"
** My Utmost for His Highest by Oswald Chambers, edited by James Reimann, © 1992 by Oswald Chambers Publications Assn., Ltd., and used by permission of Discovery House Publishers, Grand Rapids MI 49501. All rights reserved.

ACKNOWLEDGEMENTS

The writing of my memoir has reminded me once again of the joy and value of relationships, the diversity of gifts, interest, encouragement, and the time and effort it takes when pursuing a goal. The people I acknowledge in these pages, and many who are not named, have contributed to my writing by guiding, assisting, encouraging, praying and working with me. "Thank you" seems small, but it comes with magnanimity.

From the outset of telling my story, Emily, my first grandchild, encouraged me to write a selected autobiography. During coaching sessions, Barbara Murphy-Warrington stimulated me to begin writing because, "We need your story." Dorothy Clark and Joan M. Reeves held me accountable to write from my central core—a spiritual being. Veronica Huss Salpaes traveled from Washington, D.C. to Philadelphia to authenticate my work at the Hospital of the University of Pennsylvania (HUP), and Julie Winton and Bruce Goldman added their voices to the content of this book.

When I originally thought these memories would be recorded because of our family struggle with Alzheimer's disease, Donald A. Cramp readily agreed to write a preface which now introduces that section of this work. Wendy Campbell, President of the Southeastern Chapter of the Alzheimer's Association, validated my experience with Alzheimer's disease, and Bret Perkins read and offered advice for the book.

Dr. Renée C. Fox and Dr. Arnold B. (Bud) Relman, who you will meet in the content, read the entire manuscript. Renée helped me to refocus content in earlier drafts and offered language which strengthened this book. Bud offered publication advice.

Four people have been constantly working with me over three or more years, David Black, Chris Hall, L. Armstead Edwards and Abby Brisbon. Before David knew the content of the book, he honored me with the commitment to write a foreword and to be with me through publication. Chris Hall has given detailed attention to my story, reading the pages as he traveled the globe doing his University work. Chris sat beside me, pencil in hand, clarifying sentences, changing words, and encouraging me to try again. L. Armstead Edwards has been a constant presence of encouragement, assuring me that my story is worth the energy it took to write it all down. And, Abby read every draft with quiet excitement, giving attention to grammar and sentence structure, and always giving me love.

Without Mary Tutt Garrett, there would not be a book. Mary has spent three years, almost weekly, giving me encouragement, love and work. Mary has typed, re-typed and formatted my changes, incorporated the edits from others, made her own, and coordinated efforts from all of us, presenting an accurate, beautiful document each time. She has researched the Scriptures, offered unintrusive advice, and patience. Mary is my partner in this work.

Finally, Edgar and Nancy have encouraged me to take my time, to rest, and to leave for them my legacy.

To my family, Mary, and dear friends, thank you, from a grateful heart.

Delores Flynn Brisbon

ABOUT THE AUTHOR

Delores Flynn Brisbon is a community and church leader and seasoned executive. A widow, mother of two adult children and grandmother of three grandchildren, Delores is an Elder in the First Presbyterian Church in Philadelphia. Over a forty-year period, Delores has served a significant number of non-profit organizations. Currently, she serves the Board of Trustees of Eastern University, St. Davids, Pennsylvania; Mercy Health System of Southeastern Pennsylvania and Presby Inspired Life and the Board of Directors of the Presbyterian Community Ministries of Delaware Valley.

Her professional career spans more than fifty years across three health care institutions. Delores is a retired Chief Operating Officer of the Hospital of the University of Pennsylvania, the first African American to have been appointed to that position. She currently serves as a governance mentor for INTRUST—a service of the Association of Boards in Theological Education.

Delores lives in Philadelphia, Pennsylvania.

Made in the USA
Charleston, SC
19 October 2010